Rave Reviews

"125 excellent photographs, diagrams, and an easy-to-follow text...everything you need to know to turn a shaggy little Terrier into a thing of beauty and a joy forever. Here, shown for the first time in any book, are the fine points of clipping, scissoring, stripping, plucking, care of new coats, brushing, combing, bathing, pedicuring, beard trimming, eyebrow shaping. The works. The terminology is simple, the diagrams are exact, and the close-up photographs illustrate each technique with extreme clarity."

—KENNEL REVIEW

"A book that contains a wealth of detailed data for Terrier-owners and grooming salon operators. The authors are eminently qualified in their field...[and] there are step-by-step instructions, explanations, diagrams and details of the fine points of every phase of the work."

—DOG WORLD

CLIPPING AND GROOMING YOUR TERRIER

Step by Step

BEN STONE

MARIO MIGLIORINI

PRENTICE HALL PRESS
New York   London   Toronto   Sydney   Tokyo

Prentice Hall Press
Gulf + Western Building
One Gulf + Western Plaza
New York, New York 10023

Published in 1988 by the Prentice Hall Trade Division

PRENTICE HALL Press and colophon are registered
trademarks of Simon & Schuster Inc.

Previously published by Arco Publishing, Inc.

Library of Congress Catalog Card Number: 70-127113

ISBN 0-668-05326-7

Manufactured in the United States of America

10   9   8   7   6   5   4

CONTENTS

ACKNOWLEDGMENTS

We are indebted first of all to the owners of the individual breeds because they graciously gave us permission to reproduce the pictures that are used in this book. In each case the dog selected as the photographic model is one of the foremost champions of the show ring in this country and abroad. In selecting each model, we kept our ideal for that particular breed in mind at all times. Credits are listed in the back of this book.

We are also indebted to Fred Honig for his painstaking photographic work on the dogs used in the step-by-step demonstration; to Rhona Wolinsky, for the art work; and to Dr. William Shaw, owner of the Schnauzer used in the demonstration.

INTRODUCTION

by Maxwell Riddle*

When I was asked to write an introduction for this useful and needed book, I suddenly realized what an old codger I am. Why? Because I remember the last tail biter in the dog business.

Now, terriers have long tails when they are born, and, in the not-so-recent past, it was firmly believed that you couldn't get a proper tail carriage by cutting off the tail. No. You had to bite it off.

Presumably, this stretched the tendons and kept the tail from curving over the back in squirrel fashion. But, of course, you had to bite in just the right way, or you could ruin the job.

My tail-biting friend bred Airedales about 1910, and he was one of the founders of the Western Reserve Kennel Club. Booze ruined him, but, for many years, he went about plucking terriers and, upon demand, biting off the tails of newborn puppies.

I used to hear about him as a child. Later, when I grew up and began to write about dogs, I used to send him clients—or, rather, send him *to* the clients. For he took street cars and buses and walked, carrying his little kit of grooming tools.

Tom Lindsay was an artist who lived at a time when there were many dog-grooming artists. During all my childhood I used to hear the men talking about the merits of this or that dog groomer.

"No one can set down a terrier like he does," was almost a stock phrase used to start an argument or to bring on a chorus of praise.

Today, you are apt to hear the old men say, "Grooming terriers is a lost art." But it really isn't so. There are still a few great ones. These few are the pro-

---

* Mr. Riddle is Associate Editor of *Dog World* and a syndicated newspaper columnist with columns in the *N.Y. Post, Cleveland Press,* etc; he is also an international all-breed judge.

7

fessionals. However, times have changed, and today there are fewer big kennels and more smaller ones.

There is, therefore, a need for more competent owner-groomer-handlers. Few professionals are willing to share their secrets. Most of them learned by experience while working for older groomers.

Now, at long last, Ben Stone and Mario Migliorini, professionals in a dificult trade, have produced a book which, in simple terms, will give the terrier owner all the fundamental knowledge he will need. By following the authors' instructions, terrier owners should be able to set down their dogs in acceptable fashion. And they won't have to bite off tails!

M.R.

FOREWORD

Since the phenomenal success of our book *Clipping and Grooming Your Poodle—Step by Step,* which was first published in 1965 and has gone through four editions and many printings in seven years, we have been besieged by requests for a companion book on terriers.

The book on poodles was written because there was a shortage of material on the subject. What literature did exist was of a decidedly inferior and inadequate nature. We found that there was an even greater lack of material on grooming terriers. Prior to the publication of this book there was practically nothing that could serve as a guide for either the novice or the professional working with terriers. We know because we researched the market. To the best of our knowledge much of the information presented in this book has never been published before.

Before we proceed with the step-by-step instructions, it is necessary to point out the difference between the *pet* grooming of terriers and grooming terriers for *show.*

The basic difference is that in pet grooming, clippers are used to trim the dog, while for show grooming the coat is handstripped—i.e., the hair is plucked out with the fingers or with the aid of a stripping knife.

Clipping is a far easier and faster method of trimming than stripping; however, clipping makes the dog's coat lose that coarse texture considered essential by those who prepare terriers for show. Clipping is explained in the chapters not related to show grooming. In these chapters we are concerned with the pet owners and professionals who are interested only in pet trimming, yet who wish to retain the characteristic appearance of each breed.

Most pet owners, as well as the dog grooming shops which they patronize, are not familiar with the stripping technique, nor are they particularly interested, since they have no desire to ever put their dog in the show ring and don't want to pay the higher fees involved in stripping.

For those who disapprove of clipping terriers in principle, all we can say is that thousands of dogs are clipped nonetheless and that we are simply trying to see to it that each breed is at least trimmed to correspond with the standard as much as possible and not butchered beyond recognition.

For the sake of proper organization and clarification, we have divided the book into its two natural parts—the first section is titled "Pet Grooming of Terriers" and the second is "Grooming Terriers for Show."

We have chosen the Schnauzer as our basic model because, according to the registration ratings of the American Kennel Club, the Schnauzer is the most popular of all the terriers.

As far as the step-by-step procedures of such grooming fundamentals as brushing and bathing are concerned, the techniques described in these chapters are proper for all terrier breeds.

Just as we did in *Clipping and Grooming Your Poodle,* we have once again let the photographs and diagrams do most of the talking and kept the written text to a minimum. We have also tried to keep the terminology as simple and easy-to-understand as possible for the sake of the novice, who, with a little patience and practice, will learn how to keep his pet neat and trim at all times.

We hope that the need for a book on terrier grooming has now been satisfied and that this book will provide as much pleasure and be as educational as was our book on grooming the poodle.

ABOUT THE AUTHORS

Ben Stone is the Director of the International School of Dog Grooming. For over ten years prior to opening the school, Mr. Stone and his wife Pearl, author of the best-selling *Clipping and Grooming Your Poodle* (ARCO) operated dog-grooming salons in California and New York. Together they were able to learn every phase of the business through first-hand experience. Mr. Stone has written numerous articles for dog trade publications and is an authority in the field of dog grooming.

Mario Migliorini is an American Kennel Club licensed, professional handler of all breeds and has been involved with show dogs for some twenty years. He handles dogs extensively throughout the United States, and his articles on varied aspects of dog care and training have been published regularly since 1958. Together with his wife Margaret, Mr. Migliorini has been associated in the breeding, rearing, and conditioning of many fine dogs, including Scotties, Westies, Wires, Cairns, Schnauzers, and Welsh terriers, to name only a few. He is a resident of Wyoming, Delaware, where he operates a small exclusive kennel.

ESSENTIALS OF GROOMING EQUIPMENT

DO NOT SKIMP on the quality of your tools. The less costly, inferior products in the long run can prove more expensive. Tools of better quality may cost a little more, but they will do a better job and last twice as long.

The tools illustrated on the following pages show the major pieces of grooming equipment needed by the one-dog owner or the professional with many dogs to groom. The main difference is that the owner of a single dog does not need the heavy-duty equipment of the professional. For example, the average Terrier owner who wishes to groom his own dog does not need the floor dryer for "fluff drying" but can use his wife's hair dryer. Or he can purchase an Oster Airjet Dryer in any large pet shop or department store.

Other grooming accessories such as shampoos, creme rinses, coat conditioners, etc., are mentioned throughout the body of the text.

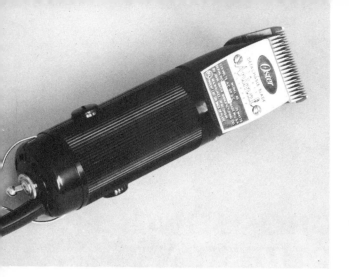

TOOLS OF THE TRADE

OSTER A-5 SMALL ANIMAL CLIPPER—
We recommend this clipper as the best in the world, for either novice or professional. A full range of blades made for this clipper can be snapped on in seconds. There is no need for screwdrivers or extra heads as with other clippers.

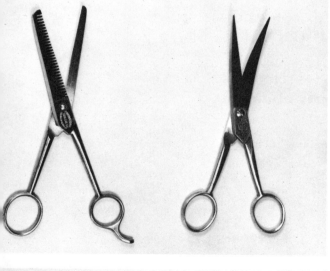

SCISSORS—BARBER & THINNING SHEARS — German-made shears are regarded as the best by the beauty and barber trade; likewise in dog groming. To do a competent job, the terrier groomer should own a pair of good German scissors and thinning shears.

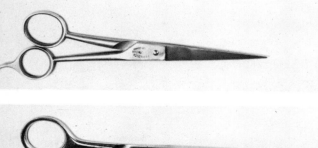

BRUSH—The "Warner" wire slicker is best for all around brushing out the coat. The wire teeth should be neither too harsh nor too soft and they should be set into a foam backing.

COMB—The best all-around comb we can recommend is one with half medium and half fine teeth. The medium side is used first to help tease out mats and tangles or to test for same. The fine side is used for final combing of the coat.

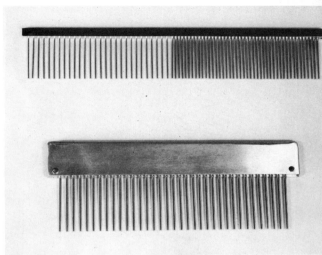

MATTING COMB—A heavy, coarse comb is best for a badly matted coat or for a coat in which foreign matter has become embedded.

NAIL CLIPPERS—The guillotine type of nail clipper illustrated here is the type to which dogs seem to object the least.

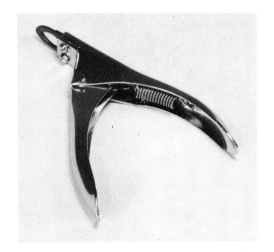

EAR PLUCKERS or HEMOSTATS — The "Kelly" Hemostats are best. This is the straight type which doesn't obstruct the vision and does a good job of plucking the excess hair from the ears.

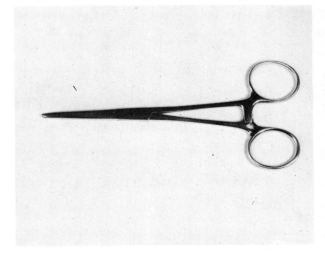

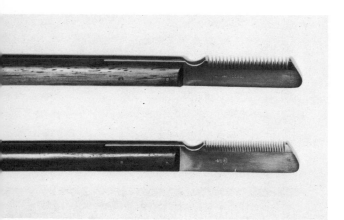

STRIPPING KNIVES—MEDIUM & FINE
—The coarse stripping knife is used for most of the areas to be stripped with the exception of the head and ears, more sensitive areas where the fine stripping knife should be used.

OSTER AIRJET HOME DRYER—This home dryer is adequate for the pet owner who just grooms his own dog. If purchased with hood, it may also be used in milady's boudoir for drying her own hair.

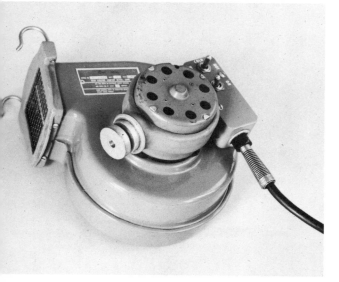

CAGE DRYER—This is a professional dryer especially constructed to be fitted on cages for drying purposes. It has a powerful air flow and dries the average dog in a matter of minutes.

FLOOR DRYER—This type is used mainly for "fluff drying," i.e., drying a damp dog and brushing at the same time where the air flow is being directed at the coat.

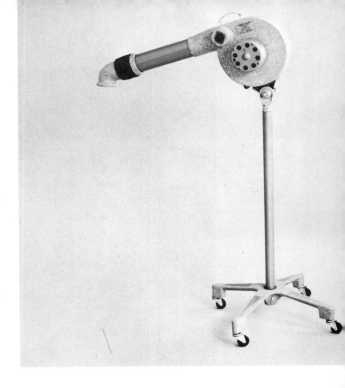

GROOMING TABLE—The traditional grooming table, usually a folding table and easily transported, is 30 inches high; the table measures 24″ x 36″. The ribbed rubber matting on top should be firmly cemented.

GROOMING POST AND LOOP—The best grooming posts are portable and can be attached to any table. The loop is placed lightly around the dog's neck to prevent the dog from moving or jumping.

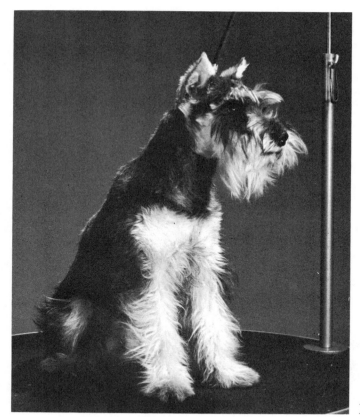

Before

After

18

PART I

Pet Grooming
of Terriers

CHAPTER 1

BRUSHING AND COMBING

Contrary to popular belief, dogs should not be bathed before brushing and combing. Instead, the coat should be completely free of all tangles and mats before being soaked with water. The reason for this seems obvious—a matted coat will become more matted when it is wet and, thus, it will be doubly hard to brush out.

Terriers, or any long-haired breed, should be brushed regularly three or four times a week. When brushing is done regularly, only a minimum amount of time is required to prepare the dog for his bath and at the same time, the dog is spared the discomfort that comes from a matted coat.

In brushing and combing it is best to start with the dog's hindquarters. This prevents the dog from seeing what is being done and, thus, gives him less reason to object. In addition, he becomes more easily accustomed to the grooming procedure. As a safeguard, place a rubber mat under the dog to keep him from slipping or sliding. When brushing, hold part of the dog's coat with one hand to relieve tension.

Begin by brushing with light downward strokes *(Photo 1-1)*. Feel for any mats or tangles with your fingers and separate these carefully so as not to pull out chunks of hair—this is especially important around the legs—then comb out tangles with the wide-toothed comb *(Photo 1-2)*. Before you continue brushing, comb with the rolling motion illustrated in the photographs. This will minimize the amount of coat damage. Once the leg furnishings have been brushed and

All step-by-step photographs by Fred Honig

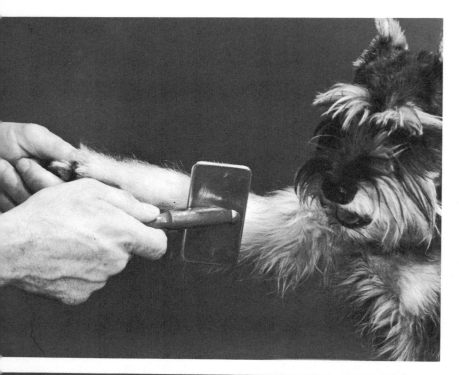

1-1.   Brushing Down

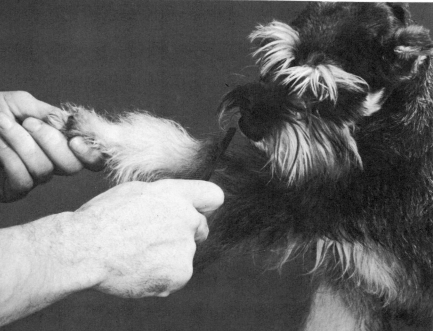

1-2.   Combing

combed thoroughly, start on the body and work to the front quarters. Lightly brush the beard and eyebrows forward and comb thoroughly *(Photos 1-3 and 1-4)*.

Never underestimate the importance of a thorough brushing and combing. It is the foundation of good grooming. Every step in dog grooming is important, but if there is one step that is more important than all others it is this one.

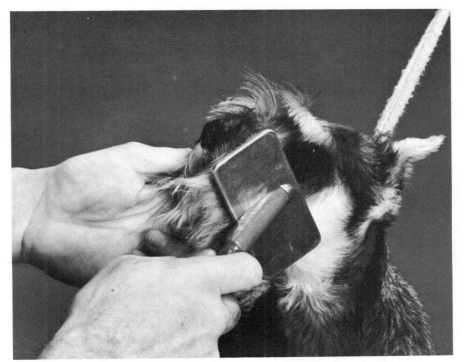

1-3. Brush Head

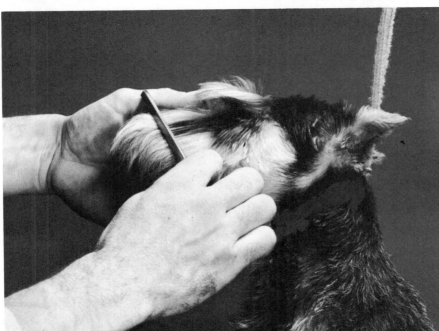

1-4. Comb Out Beard

21

CHAPTER 2

BATHING

To keep your terrier clean and free of odor, bathe him at least bi-monthly. We recommend bathing the dog at the time of his regular bi-monthly grooming since it is an essential part of the grooming process.

Prepare your materials before putting the dog in the tub. You will need a shampoo, a bristle brush, a sponge, and a towel (*Photo 2-1*). Have everything ready before you begin. It's a good idea to wear a plastic apron, since the dog

2-1. Bathing Materials

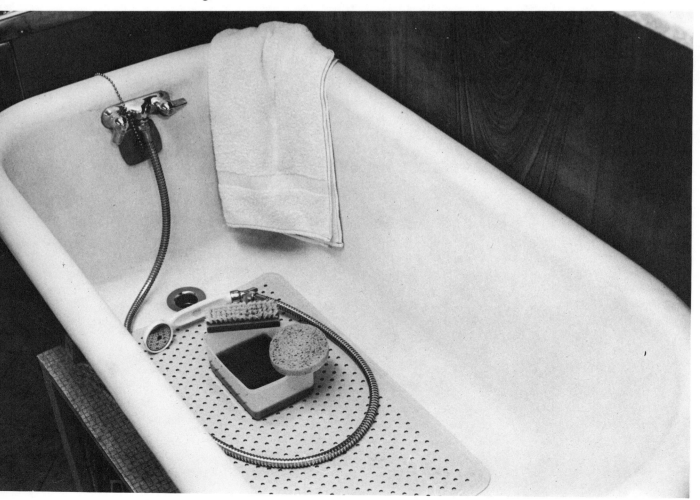

will not be choosy about the moment he decides to shake the excess water from his coat and give you a bath, too.

If you decide to use a concentrated shampoo, dilute it in a dish first and then saturate the sponge with it. Attach a hose, preferably a shower spray such as the one shown in the bathing photos, to the faucet to facilitate soaking and rinsing the dog. The water should be warm, but not hot, and should always run free, never filling the tub.

Soak the dog thoroughly, starting at the rear and working forward (*Photo 2-2*). Pay particular attention to the rectum. Most terrier coats are somewhat water resistant, so you will have to force the water with your hand through the hair to his skin while you are soaking him. Be careful of his eyes and hold your thumb against the ear canal when you wet around the dog's ears. It is better not to put cotton in his ears. Placing the thumb against the ear canal is sufficient to keep water out.

2-2.   Soaking

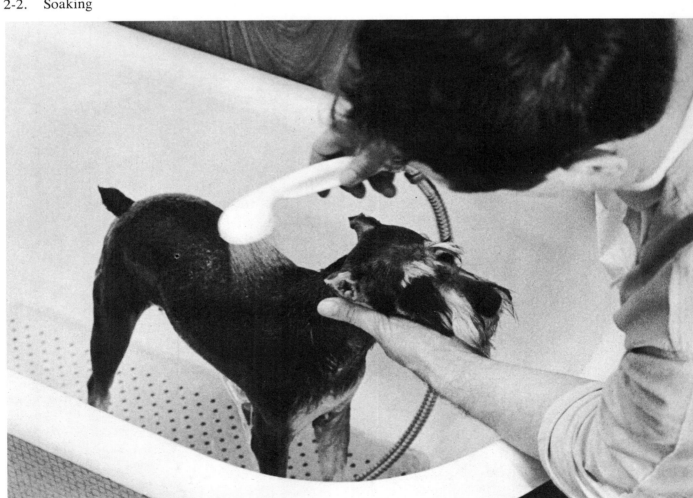

Once the dog has been completely soaked, take the shampoo-saturated sponge and begin working up a good lather. Once again, you should move from back to front and pay special attention to the rectum and the pads (the bottom of the paws). Don't be stingy with the soap (*Photo 2-3*).

When you are washing the dog's head, take special care not to get soap into his eyes. A dog will never have the proper attitude toward his bath if it becomes a torturous experience, complete with burning eyes. Use your hands rather than the sponge in this area. In fact, novices might prefer to use one of the many "no tear" baby shampoos which are now on the market.

The next step is to take a small bristle brush and, using a light, rearward motion (*Photo 2-4*), to brush the lather into the fur covering all parts of the body. Then rinse the dog off from front to rear, being especially careful of the eyes and ears. Continue rinsing until all traces of soap have been washed away.

Gently squeeze the hair on the legs, tail, ears, and all parts of the dog's body with your hands to remove excess water; then rub him briskly with the towel (*Photo 2-5*). Place the dog under a dryer and dry thoroughly before you brush and comb once again.

To keep the dog clean between groomings, simply apply a "dry" shampoo over his entire coat and towel dry.

2-3. Soaping

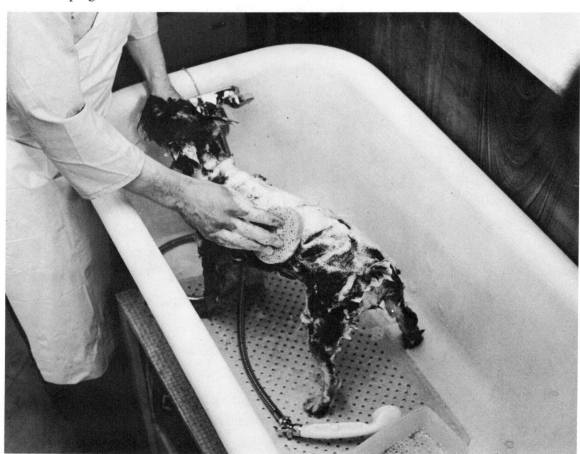

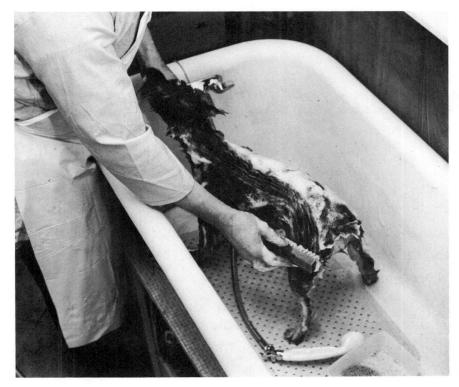

2-4. Bristle Brush

2-5. Toweling

25

CHAPTER 3

HANDLING AND CONTROL

Lack of control can lead to some very clumsy situations while you are grooming a dog. The motto of our school is "Firmness plus Gentleness." While an obedient dog is a prerequisite to good grooming, the entire procedure also requires a handler who is both firm and gentle. Firmness does not mean roughness or brutality, but the dog must know who is the master and that his grooming period is not a time for play or petting.

Think in terms of training a child. With a youngster we can be both firm in our demands and gentle in our manner of enforcing them. Of course, the owner of a spoiled dog has one advantage over the parents of a spoiled child —the dog in need of special correction can be referred to a dog obedience trainer; to the spoiled child's parents, we can offer only sympathy.

The question of handling and control, or the proper combination of firmness and gentleness, is not as simple as it might seem, especially for the novice who is making his first attempts at grooming a dog. The tendency is to let the dog have his own way, but the novice will soon learn that grooming can then become an ordeal rather than a pleasant experience.

What is the right combination of firmness and gentleness? There can be no precise answer, and we can only say that experience may be the best teacher.

The average dog should become accustomed to being groomed while he is still a puppy, and, therefore, should not present a problem. In those exceptional cases where the dog has become extremely spoiled and unmanageable or has been mistreated, it may be impossible to do a good grooming job.

CONTROLLING YOUR DOG ON THE TABLE

When the dog is on the grooming table (and there should always be a rubber mat on the table top) you can control him best by holding him lightly with your hand between his rear legs. If the dog moves or attempts to sit down,

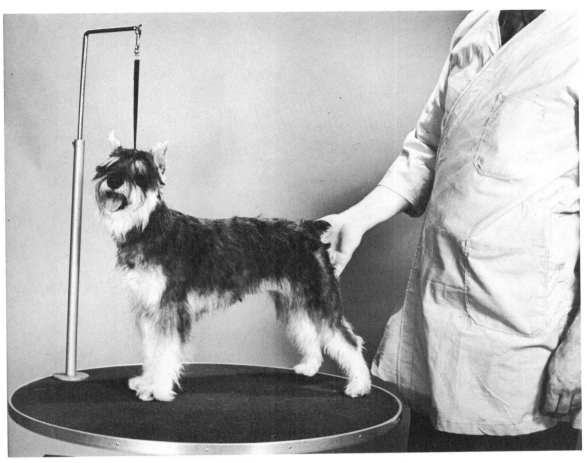

3-1. Post and Loop

gentle pressure will bring him back into the right position. Don't position the dog by lifting him under the stomach, as this will cause him to hump up.

You cannot achieve maximum control unless you make certain that both you and the dog are comfortable. If either of you is not comfortable during any part of the grooming process, the dog cannot be handled properly. A good deal of common sense must enter into this relationship. For example, during each stage of the grooming there are logical times for either the dog or you to sit down. Whenever this is possible, do so. But the dog must also stand when standing is required and stay when so commanded.

The use of the grooming post and loop is frequently necessary and can be a great aid to better handling and control (*Photo 3-1*).

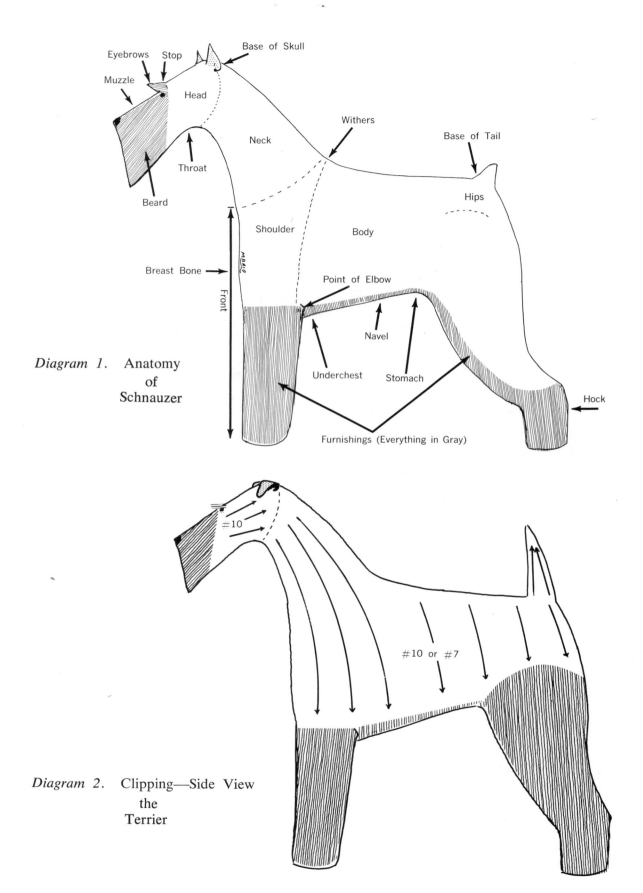

Eyebrows Stop   Base of Skull

Muzzle

Head

Base of Tail

Throat

Neck

Withers

Beard

Hips

Shoulder

Body

Breast Bone

Front

Point of Elbow

Navel

Underchest   Stomach

Hock

Furnishings (Everything in Gray)

Diagram 1. Anatomy
of
Schnauzer

#10

#10 or #7

Diagram 2. Clipping—Side View
the
Terrier

THE LONG-LEGGED TERRIERS

SCHNAUZER   WELSH   AIREDALE

WIRE FOX   LAKELAND   IRISH

The Schnauzer was chosen as the model for pet grooming simply because it is the most popular of all the terriers. With the exception of the headpiece, which is trimmed to give each breed its own characteristic expression, the above terriers can all be groomed in similar fashion.

We will start by clipping the body, since this is the easiest part of the job.

4-1. Start of Clipping

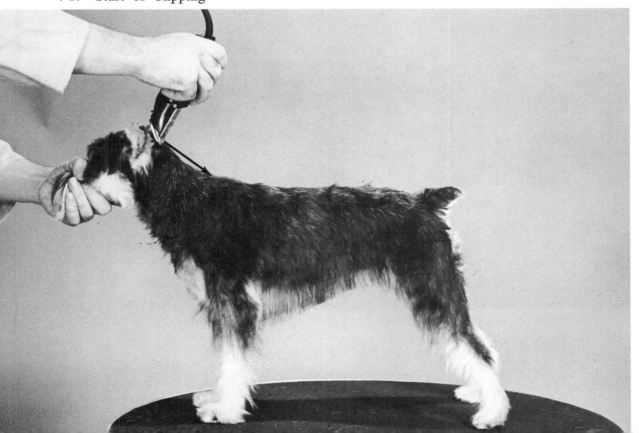

CLIPPING

Body Pattern

A No. 10 or No. 7 blade can be used, the No. 10 giving a freshly stripped appearance and the No. 7 a more fully coated look. With the "Oster" blades for the model A2 or A5 clipper, the higher the number the closer the clip. In this demonstration, we are using the No. 7 blade for the body pattern.

From the base of the skull (*Photo 4-1*), clip down the neck to the withers

4-2. Clipping Down Back

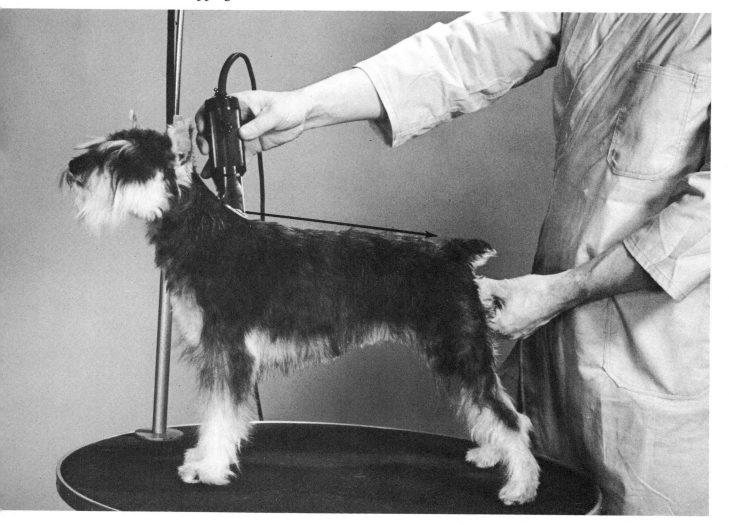

(shoulders) (*Photo 4-2*) and using the spine as a guideline, go along the back to the base of the tail. Next, clip down the side of the neck, and over the withers to the elbow (*Photo 4-3*). Starting at the withers, clip over the body with long sweeping strokes. Always work in the direction of the coat and follow the contour of the dog along an inclining line from the front of the elbow to the hips. Use slightly overlapping strokes. The legs and chest remain untouched by the clippers.

4-3.   Clipping to Elbow

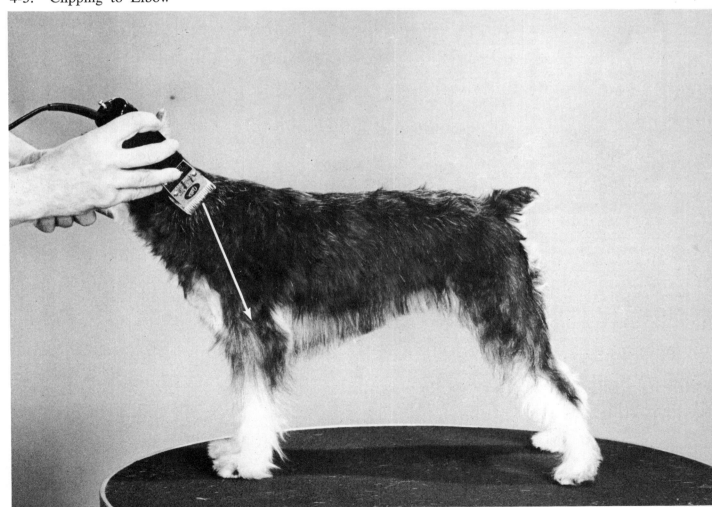

Unlike the other terriers, the Schnauzer's rear legs are clipped (*Diagram 3, Photo 4-4*). Care must be taken to leave a clearly defined fringe on the fore-part of the legs and curving back to just above the hock (*Diagram 4*). In most Schnauzers this area is outlined by white hair.

4-4.   Clipping Schnauzer's Rear Legs

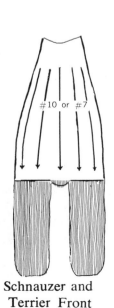
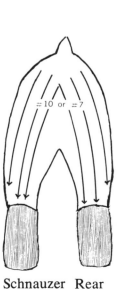
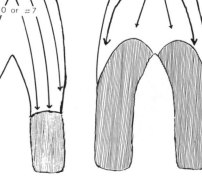

Schnauzer and
Terrier Front

Schnauzer Rear

Terrier Rear

Diagram 3.   Clipping—
Rear and Front View

Neck and Forechest

Clip from the throat down the front part of neck and forechest to a point level with the elbows. This will give a clean, straight line. Use the same blade as you did on the body (*Photo 4-5*).

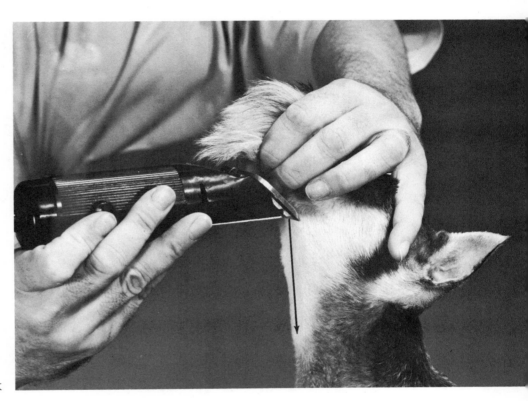

4-5.   Clipping Down Neck

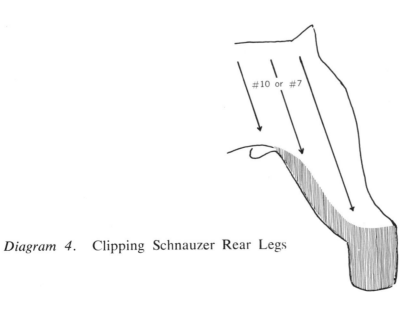

#10 or #7

Diagram 4.   Clipping Schnauzer Rear Legs

33

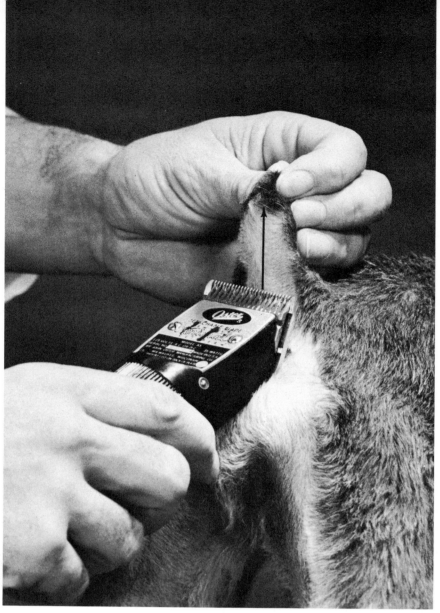

4-6. Clipping Tail

Tail

Still using the same blade, clip from the base to the tip of the tail (*Photo 4-6*), both the front and the back. Unless the tail has been docked short, you should try to achieve a round, slightly tapered effect (*Diagram 5*).

Diagram 5. Terrier Tails

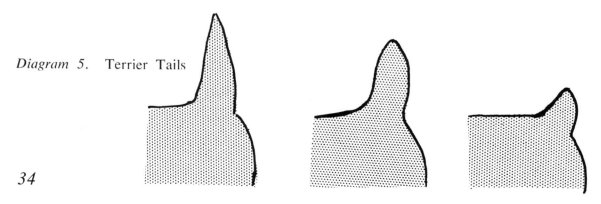

34

Underbelly

Using a No. 10 blade, clip the stomach up to the navel. Take care not to go beyond this area (*Photo 4-7*). Then, still using the No. 10 blade, trim the excess hair on the penis of the male dog.

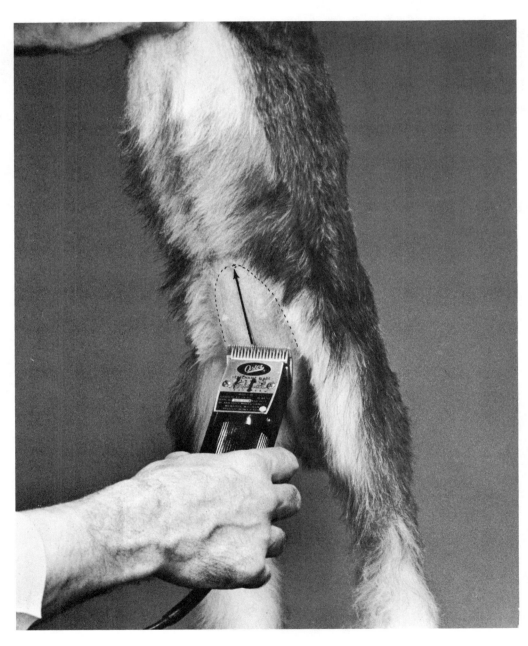

4-7. Clipping Stomach

4-8. Clipping Skull

4-9. Clipping Side of Head

Head

Comb the hair on the face forward from a line just above the eyebrows to the corners of the mouth. Use a No. 10 blade and clip the head back from above the eyebrows to the base of the skull (*Photo 4-8*), then from the outer corner of the eye (on the Schnauzer and Scottish terrier from the outer edge of eyebrow) to the base of the ear (*Photo 4-9*), and from the corners of the mouth back to form a "V" at the throat (*Photo 4-10*). Photo 4-10 shows the direction in which these areas must be clipped.

4-10. Clipping Head and Throat

Ears

Clip the front (*Photo 4-11*) and back (*Photo 4-12*) of the ears with a No. 10 or No. 15 blade for a closer finish. Always clip from the center toward the outer edges of the ear and away from the head. Do not clip against the grain or along the edges of the ears.

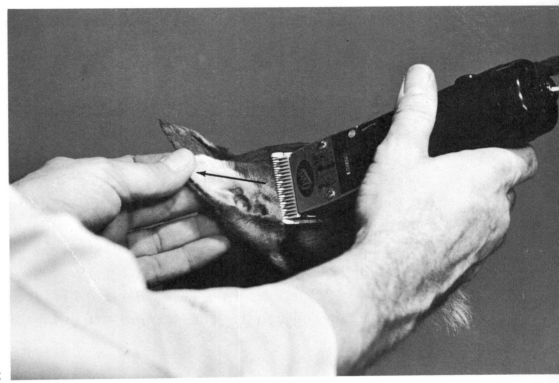

4-11. Clipping Ears, Front

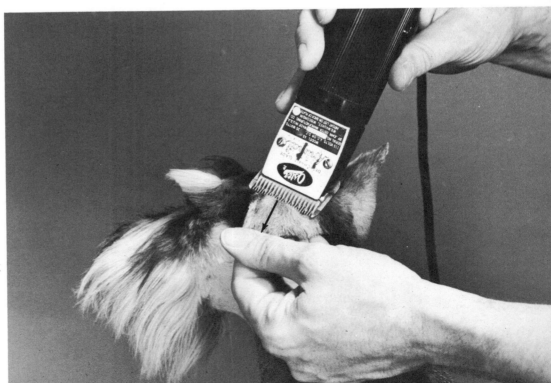

4-12. Clipping Ears, Back

SCISSORING

Head

Shaping terrier heads, especially the eyebrows and beard, will do a great deal to contribute to the correct expression of each breed. This can be done only by proper scissoring.

It might help the novice to remember that the eyebrows of a Schnauzer or Scottie should resemble a shade or visor extending diagonally from the outer corner to the inner edge of the eyes and divided at the stop to form two right angle triangles ◺◿ with the perpendicular lines on the inside and approximately parallel.

Eyebrows

Comb the eyebrows directly forward, using a long stroke to include the beard (*Photo 4-13*); then, with the tips of the straight-edged scissors held open to the width of the inner corner of the dog's eyes, insert the points gently through the center of the eyebrows at the stop (*Photo 4-14*). Keeping the shears parallel with the top of the muzzle, cut away the surplus hair, thus separating the eyebrows. Trim the outer edges of the eyebrows so that they are level with the side of the head (*Photo 4-15*); then cut them diagonally from the outer edge to the center (*Photo 4-16*) with a single stroke. Take care

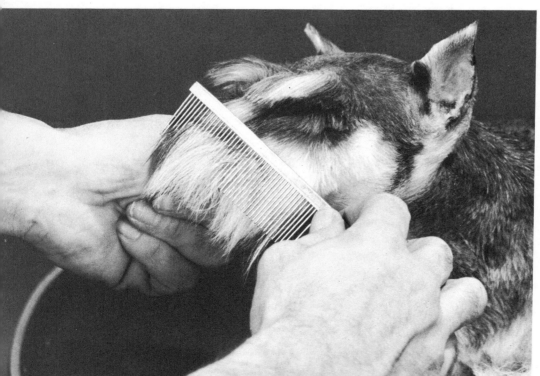

4-13.   Combing Head

4-14.   Scissoring at Stop

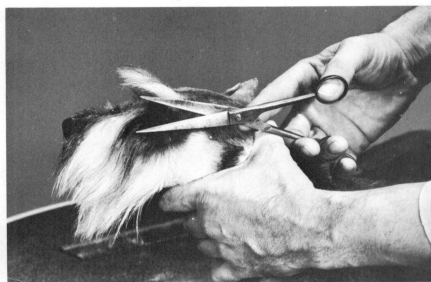

4-15.   Scissoring Outer Eyebrows

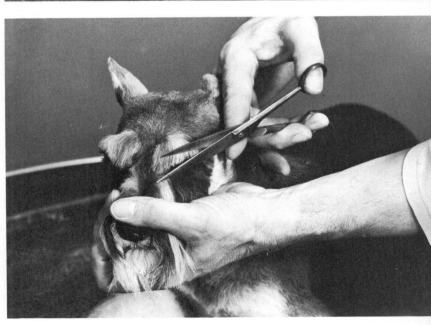

4-16.   Scissoring Diagonally

to insure that the dog does not move during this operation. Finally, using a line from the center of the stop to the inner corner of the eye (*Photo 4-17*), cut an inverted "V" between the eyebrows. This should result in properly groomed Schnauzer eyebrows (*Photo 4-18*).

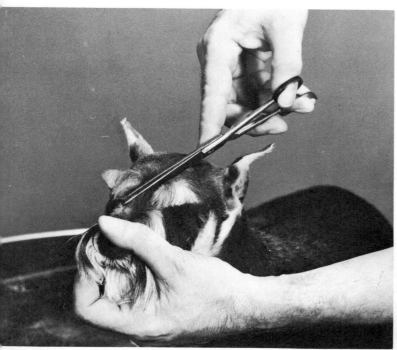

4-17.   Scissoring Inverted "V"

4-18.   Well-Groomed Eyebrows

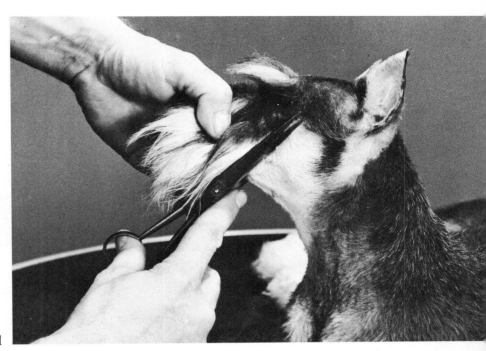

4-19.   Holding Beard

Beard

Comb the beard forward and grasp both the beard and the muzzle (*Photo 4-19*); then cut with straight-edged shears along a line extending from the corner of the mouth to the corner of the eyebrow (*Photo 4-20*). As illustrated, remove all excess hair that cannot be held.

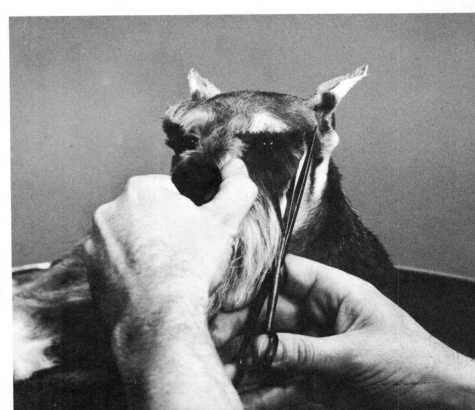

4-20.   Scissoring Excess Beard

Ears

Trim around the outer edges of the ear (*Photo 4-21*) with scissors while holding the ear straight with your fingers (*Photo 4-22*). Scissor very carefully to avoid cutting the ear itself.

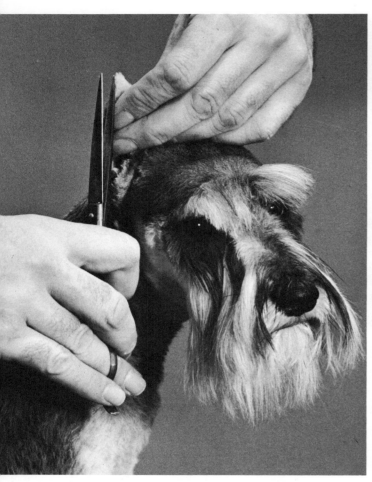 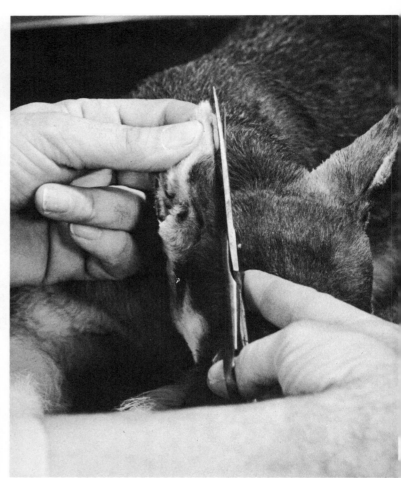

4-21.   Scissoring Outer Edges of Ear   4-22.   Scissoring Ear

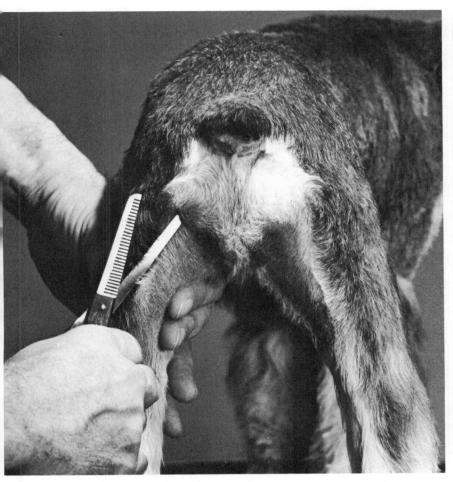

4-23.   Thinning Shears on Legs

4-24.   Front Legs Straight

Legs

Brush out the furnishings and use thinning shears to blend the furnishings and body coat as well as to shape and finish off the legs (*Photo 4-23*) and lower part of chest. The front legs should be made to appear as round and as straight as possible (*Photo 4-24*). As a rule, a very little trimming is necessary for the front part of the legs.

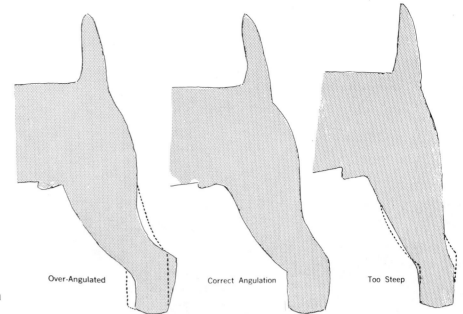

Diagram 6. Angulation

Over-Angulated   Correct Angulation   Too Steep

The hindquarters should be scissored evenly with the contour of the leg, and the hair on the front should remain slightly longer than the hair on the back so that there is a moderate degree of angulation (*Diagram 6*). Using the No. 10 blade, hold the clipper diagonally across the inner corner of the leg as illustrated (*Photo 4-25*) and clip downward to the hock. Trim the hair from both the inside and the outside of the leg simultaneously to leave a clearly defined line and give the rear quarters a clean archlike appearance (*Photo 4-26*). The

4-25.   Trimming Hindquarters

4-26.   Legs Archlike

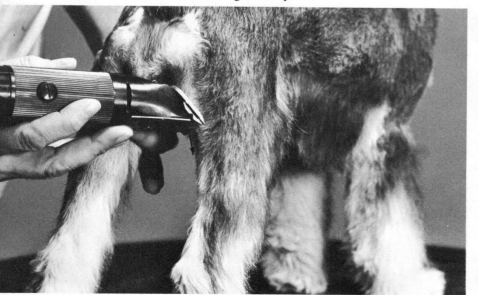

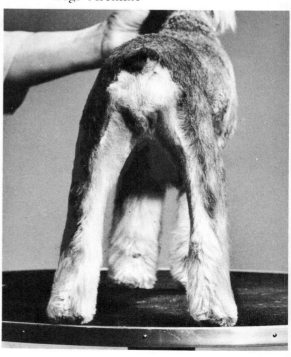

hocks should be round and straight to correspond with the front legs as much as possible. The feet should be scissored to look round and compact.

Underchest

The hair on the underchest should be scissored so that it follows the contour of the body. It should incline gently from the point of the elbow and form a slight tuckup at the loin. To accomplish this, extend the front leg forward, bringing the elbow into a right angle position, and scissor toward the rear along the line indicated (*Photo 4-27*); then repeat on the opposite side. Thinning shears may be used instead of regular scissors for a smoother effect.

4-27. Scissoring Underchest

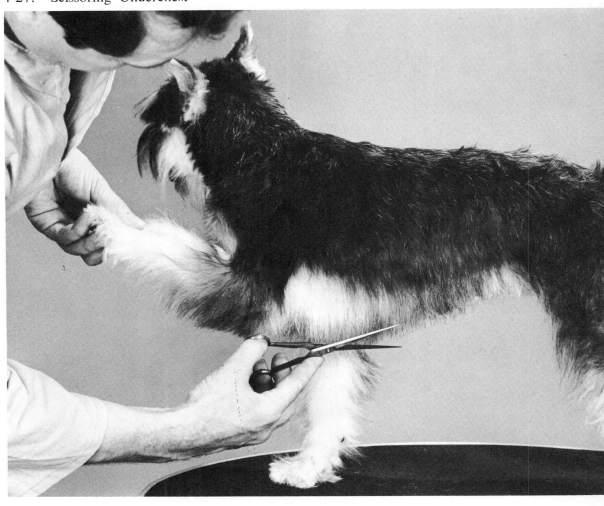

Feet

Comb out the feet and gently remove any mats between the toes. Holding a foot, cut away the hair between the pads (*Photo 4-28*), with scissors, or clipper using a No. 10 blade.

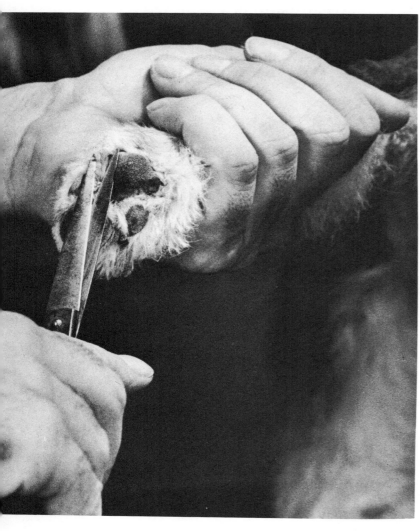

4-28. Scissoring Pads

CHAPTER 5

THE OTHER TERRIERS

WIRE FOX   WELSH   IRISH   AIREDALE

As far as the pet groomer is concerned, the principal difference between the terriers is the shape and size of the head, which varies in length and thickness among both breeds and individuals. Consequently, even if all heads were trimmed the same way, there would still be variations in appearance. However, there are different variations which should be used when you trim heads, and these variations help create the expression which has become characteristic of each breed.

Diagram 7. Wire Fox Terrier

The Wire Fox, Welsh, Irish, and Airedale terrier heads should be made to look as long and clean as possible (*Diagram 7*). After clipping along the lines indicated for the Schnauzer in the previous chapter, use thinning shears to thin and shape the beard as necessary. Clip the front and back of the ears with blade No. 10 or 15 and tidy the edges with scissors. Eyebrows should be small, divided, as previously explained in the Schnauzer section, and triangular-shaped. Excess hair on top of the muzzle should be trimmed with thinning shears or, in extreme cases, clipped with a No. 10 blade from below the eyebrows.

LAKELAND

The Lakeland terrier differs from the other above named terrier breeds in that it does not usually have divided eyebrows but has instead a fall in the middle of the brow which blends into the hair on top of the muzzle to give it strength (*Diagram 8*). The eyebrows should be scissored diagonally from the outer corner to the inner corner of the eye so that the eye is exposed.

The ears should be clipped and scissored just as they are for the other terriers.

Diagram 8. Lakeland Head

48

CHAPTER 6

THE SHORT-LEGGED TERRIERS

SCOTTISH SEALYHAM WEST HIGHLAND WHITE

One of the most important things when clipping a short-legged terrier is the necessity of retaining a squat, solid appearance. The basic procedure is similar to that used for the long-legged breeds, but careful attention should be given to the diagrams, which illustrate the distinctive features that characterize each breed. Note the full beard, overhanging eyebrows, and tufted ears of the Scottie (*below*); the full face and heavy, undivided eyebrows of the Sealy (*Diagram 9*); the full head and lack of eyebrow definition of the Westie (*Diagram 10*). In addition, unlike their taller cousins, these terriers retain a natural, skirted appearance and, thus, their legs and underparts need not be shaped or fashioned.

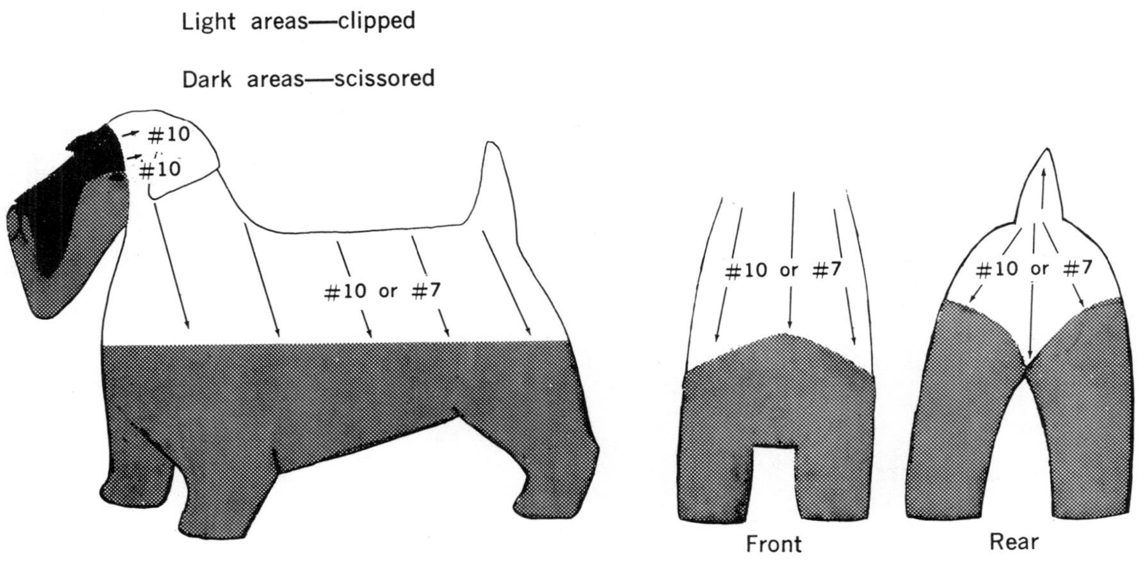
Light areas—clipped
Dark areas—scissored
#10
#10
#10 or #7
#10 or #7
#10 or #7
Front
Rear

Diagram 9. Sealy

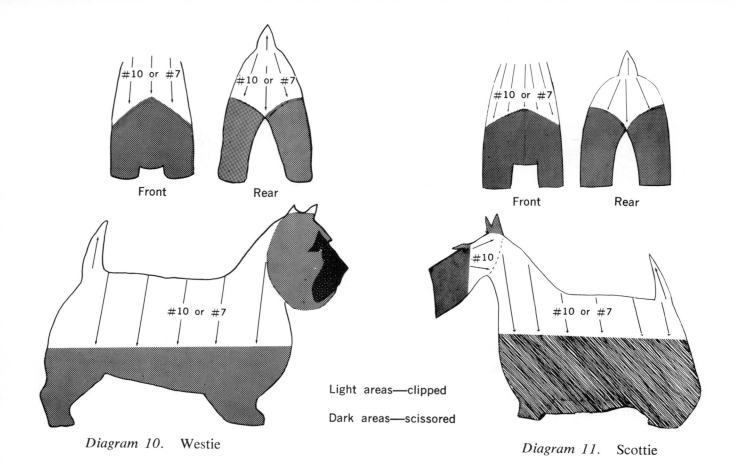

Front   Rear

Front   Rear

Light areas—clipped

Dark areas—scissored

Diagram 10. Westie

Diagram 11. Scottie

CLIPPING

Body Pattern

Use a No. 10 or a No. 7 blade for the short-legged terrier, just as you do for the long-legged ones (*Diagram 11*). Using the spine as a guideline, clip down the back of the neck from the base of the skull to the withers and from the withers to the base of the tail. Then clip down the side of the neck to the point of the shoulder, approximately midway between the withers and the elbow. Continue clipping over the body with long sweeping strokes which follow the contour of the dog. Work in the direction of the lay of the coat, from front to back along a line extending from the point of the shoulder to the point of the rump (*Diagram 12*).

Neck and Forechest

Still with the same blade, clip from the front part of the neck to the point of the sternum, or breastbone.

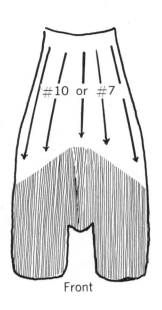
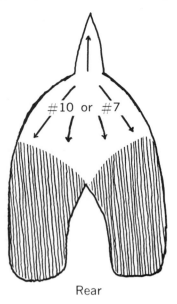

Diagram 12. Short-Legged Terriers

#10 or #7

#10 or #7

Front

Rear

Tail

Working from base to tip, clip both the front and the back of the tail for a round, slightly tapered effect, using the same blade as on the body.

Scottie Head

To clip a Scottie's head (*Diagram 13*), comb the hair on the face forward from a line just above the eyebrows and extending to the corners of the mouth. Hold the dog gently by the muzzle; then, using a No. 10 blade, clip the head back from above the eyebrows to the base of the skull, from the outer edge of the eyebrows to the base of the ear, and from the corners of the mouth back to the throat.

Diagram 13. Scottish Terrier

51

Scottie Ears

The way a Scottish terrier's ears are trimmed makes a unique contribution to its expression. A pompon of hair is left attached to the head and to the front inner edge of the ear. To produce this effect, clip the back of the ear first and then clip the front, taking care to clean off the outer edge and only the upper half of the inside edge. Scissor carefully around the ear but only midway down on the inside. Then fold the top half of the ear down and, with scissors, trim surplus hair in a straight line level with the folded edge. Repeat for opposite ear.

The scissoring of the Scottie eyebrows is the same as that for the Schnauzer.

Sealy Head and Ears

The Sealyham terrier face should be left very full. Preferably the eyebrows remain undivided, although they must be trimmed diagonally on either side to expose the eye. The underbeard stays very full and this, coupled with the heavy brow, creates a rounded effect (*Diagram 14*). Clip ears front and back with a No. 10 blade and trim with scissors.

Diagram 14. Sealyham

Diagram 15. West Highland White

West Highland White Head and Ears

The Westie head is never clipped (*Diagram 15*); any tidying that may be necessary should be done with thinning shears. It is correct to shape the head so that it looks very round when viewed from the front and resembles two soup plates, one inverted upon the other, when viewed from the side. The upper half of the ears should be clipped front and back with a No. 10 blade and the edges neatly scissored. Excess hair around the eyes can be plucked out with the fingers.

Heads and Ears of Other Terrier Breeds

Those short-legged terriers which are not specifically mentioned can be trimmed in the same manner as the Westie, except that their ears should be clipped to the base.

PART II

Grooming Terriers for Show

CHAPTER 7

THE LONG-LEGGED TERRIERS (STRIPPING AND PLUCKING)

| WIRE FOX | WELSH | AIREDALE |
| SCHNAUZER | LAKELAND | IRISH |

The Wire Fox terrier was used as the model for show grooming because it is considered the classical terrier. With the exception of the headpiece, all the above terriers can be groomed in similar fashion.

STRIPPING AND PLUCKING

Terriers that will compete in dog shows must be hand-stripped. You can do this either with the aid of a stripping knife or by plucking, i.e., picking the hair out with your fingers.

Until recently it was unheard of to clip a terrier, but today, even at dog shows, one frequently sees thinning shears, razor-combs, and clippers being used. However, as this practice invariably damages the texture of the coat and, consequently, reduces the individual's chances of winning against more pro-

The Wire Fox, the Classical Terrier—"Piper"

fessionally "put down" competition, it is not to be recommended for the serious-minded exhibitor.

In order to give completely detailed, step-by-step instructions for preparing each of the various terriers for show, we would have to write a separate book on every breed. For the purposes of this book, however, we thought it best to generalize as much as possible in order to avoid confusing the beginner. This is also why we used the Schnauzer and the Wire Fox, by far the most popular of all the terrier breeds, as our models.

The majority of people who hand-strip their dogs do so in the hope of showing them. However, those who are not interested in showing but simply wish to strip their dogs so that the coats will retain the correct characteristics, should follow the same process, although they can, of course, pay less attention to minor details and coat maintenance.

If you are going to successfully prepare a dog for show, you must become a combination hairdresser and make-up artist. You should give ample consideration to the dog's conformation, or to the way his physical structure conforms to the American Kennel Club's standard for that breed, and you must learn to exploit the maximum show potential of each dog. Before you actually begin to work on your dog, it is essential that you read the breed standard, make a habit of seeing show winners in the ring, and try to become as familiar with your subject as possible. We have never met a handler who felt that he or she had a surplus of knowledge.

Acquiring a harsh, tight coat on a terrier takes time and patience. "A strong arm and a weak mind" was once a popular adage. Unfortunately, it's not quite that simple! The average period of time required to grow and build a good coat is around eight weeks; however, this will vary both among breeds and among individual dogs. There are no hard and fast rules, and everyone must learn by trial and error how long it will take to bring any one particular dog to its peak condition.

In order to be successfully stripped, a terrier's coat must be what professional groomers refer to as "blown"—i.e., it must have grown out so that it is virtually dead. When a coat is in this condition, it will stand out from the body, be very wavy, and so loose that strands of hair can be easily plucked out with the fingers without apparent discomfort to the dog. Once the coat has blown, the dog does not have to be stripped immediately, but can be left "in the rough" for several weeks if necessary.

The day before you start stripping your terrier, it is advisable to "chalk" the parts to be stripped (*Diagram 16*). This helps dry the oils from the coat and makes it easier to hold. Use one of the commercial chalk blocks for easy application over the specified area, or in the event that chalk in block form is not readily available, a small quantity of calcium carbonate can be obtained from almost any drug store.

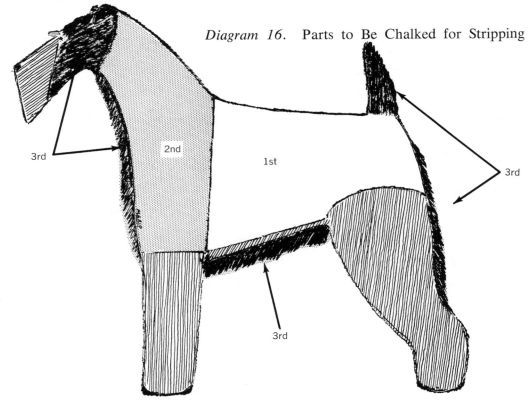

Diagram 16. Parts to Be Chalked for Stripping

3rd

2nd

1st

3rd

3rd

56

The initial stripping can be done in three stages, seven days to two weeks apart, depending on the breed. The body coat is always stripped off first. In the second stage the neck and shoulders are stripped, and the third stage includes the head, ears, front, tail, and rear. The job is divided this way because the rate of growth of the hair varies on different parts of the body, and staggered stripping is the best established method of achieving a uniform coat at showtime.

The dog should be placed on a suitably elevated surface, ideally a grooming table equipped with a restraining post and loop, to enable you to handle and control him with a minimum of effort.

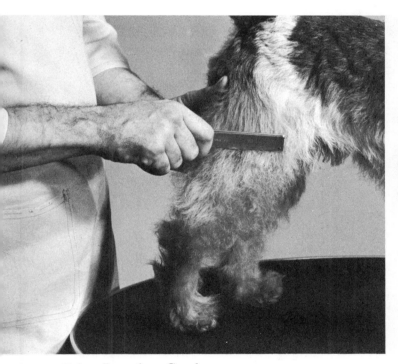 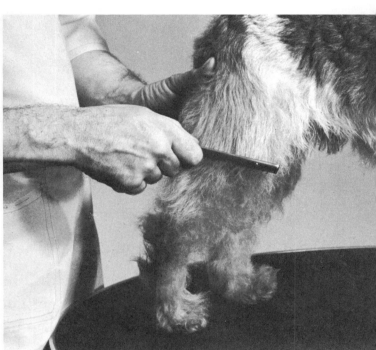

7-1.   Inserting Comb   7-2.   Levering Comb

Combing

The first step is to comb out the coat with a wide-toothed comb such as the "Resco" #80. In order to minimize damage to the furnishings and undercoat, insert the comb diagonally into the hair (*Photo 7-1*), and lever it into perpendicular position (*Photo 7-2*); then, without withdrawing the teeth, work the comb through the coat. Use a gentle, rolling motion to advance the comb

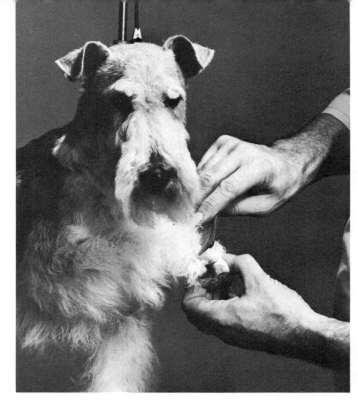

7-3. Combing Hair Up

and separate snarls and continue until the dog has been completely combed out. Separate the more stubborn knots with your fingers. Repeat the process with the coarse side of a regular comb and remember to comb the hair *up* from in between the toes (*Photo 7-3*).

Stripping the Body—Step by Step

On the long-legged terriers the initial area to be stripped should extend from the withers to the base of the tail, down the side of the body to a line not lower than the elbow. Do not strip the shoulders at this time. Work back along an inclining line from the point of the elbow, along the flank, and to the hips. Leave the hair on the underchest.

Start by standing slightly to the rear and to one side, the right side if you are right-handed and the opposite side if you are left-handed, of the dog. Brace the hand nearest the dog on the back of its neck and start stripping out the coat from behind the shoulder, working toward the tail.

Hold the stripping knife as illustrated (*Photo 7-4*) and, as if you were thumbing through the pages of a book, ruff a small amount of the coat with your thumb. Leaving your thumb under the displaced hair and bringing the stripping knife into contact with your thumb by gently clenching your hand,

58

trap the hair between the blade and your thumb (*Photo 7-5*) and pull the hair out with a firm, plucking motion in the same direction as the growth of the coat. Photo 7-6 shows the amount of hair to be removed. Do not cut the coat with the blade. This may happen if you make an exaggerated wrist movement after the hair has been trapped under your thumb. Follow Diagram 16 closely when you strip the terrier parts. Strip only the body area at this time, as shown.

7-4.   Holding Stripping Knife

7-5.   Trapping the Hair

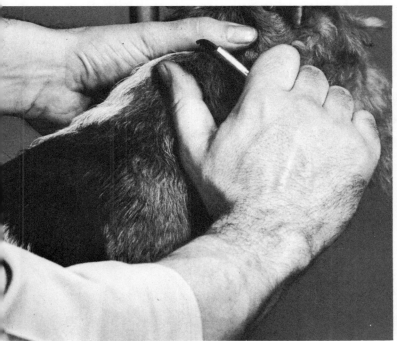

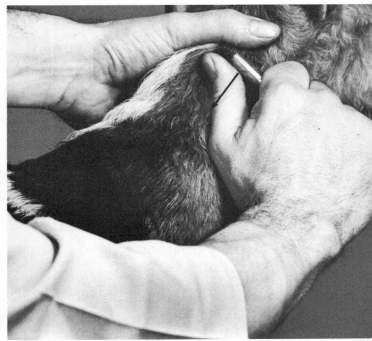

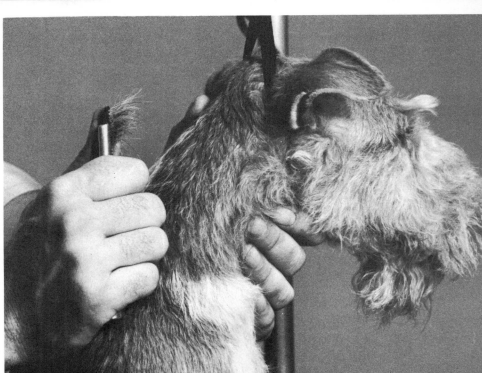

7-6.   Amount of Hair Removed

Neck and Shoulders

Approximately ten to fourteen days after stripping the body, strip off the neck and shoulders by using the same technique described for the body; then, about one week later, strip off the remaining areas.

Head and Ears

The head and ears are perhaps the most sensitive areas to strip, and, in these areas, best results can be obtained by carefully plucking the hair out with your fingers. Standing in front of the dog, ruff very small amounts by scratching lightly with your forefinger and, using the same wrist action you use when dealing cards, pluck out the hair with your forefinger and thumb. Use a fine stripper if you are unable to get the job done without one, but always lift the hair out by the ends, taking care not to pinch the skin or cut the dog.

Front, Tail, and Rear

Finally strip off the front, tail, and rear, including the backs of the legs. You may need someone to hold up the hindquarters while you are working on this area.

Unlike the other terriers, the Schnauzer's rear legs need to be stripped at the same time as the body. Care must be taken to leave a clearly defined fringe on the forepart of the legs and curving back to just above the hock.

When you are stripping a dog, a strategically placed mirror will enable you to view your progress from both sides simultaneously. During the entire operation the novice groomer should test to make sure that the coat is being stripped and not cut. This is done by stroking the stripped area against the grain—if you feel sharp stubble you are not doing a good job because the area should be covered only by soft downy undercoat, the harsh top coat having been removed by the roots.

After you have stripped a designated body area, the skin will probably look rather pink and irritated. Apply either baby oil or any preferred coat oil to soothe the skin and prevent drying and flaking. There is no need to strip out the undercoat at this time.

BATHING

When the final phase of stripping has been completed, the dog can be bathed. Before you put the dog into the bathtub, set out shampoo ("Mr. Groom" is recommended), a bristle brush, a sponge, and a towel. As bathing is not a regular occurrence for your terrier, you should wear a plastic apron to protect your clothes. Then, using only tepid water, soak the dog thoroughly and apply shampoo with the sponge, soaping from the back to the front and working up a good lather. Pay particular attention to the rectum and the pads and be careful not to get soap into the dog's eyes and ears when you are sponging his head. Next, take a small bristle brush and, with a light, downward stroke, brush soap into the furnishings. Rinse the dog and continue rinsing until all traces of soap have been washed off. Gently squeeze the hair on the legs, on the beard, and all parts of the dog's body with your hands to remove excess water before you rub him briskly with a towel and place him in a warm spot to dry. After the dog is thoroughly dry, comb and brush him as previously described.

Since the bathing procedure here is essentially the same as for bathing pets, the reader should also refer to Chapter 2.

CHAPTER 8

BUILDING THE COAT

After your dog has been completely stripped, there is little to do for a couple of weeks, apart from keeping the furnishings in shape and brushing lightly with a natural bristle brush or hound glove two or three times a week. This is the time to concentrate on getting him into good physical condition.

When the new coat begins to appear, usually in about three or four weeks, start stripping out the undercoat, but take care not to strip out the new coat along with it.

Since the hair on the head, neck, and shoulders grows far more rapidly than it does on the body, these areas must be gently restripped every month or so. In the meantime the body coat should be "rolled." This is done by grasping the ends of hair between your first two fingers and thumb and snapping your fingers. This forces the hair to roll between your fingers and thumb so that small amounts of dead, loose, or unwanted hair come out, thus promoting new, staggered growth.

8-1. Carding

8-2. Following Contour

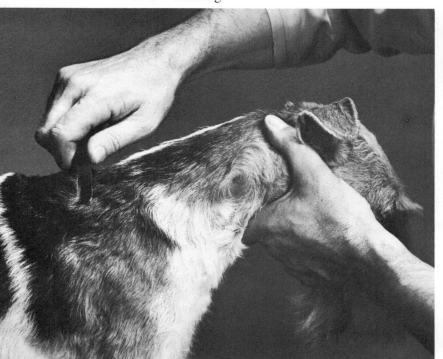

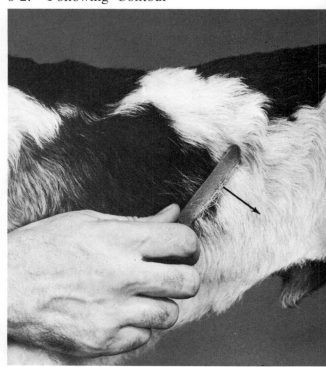

"Carding," which means combing or raking through the coat to remove excess undercoat, should also be introduced at about this time. You should stand in front of the dog and lay the blade of your stripping knife flat on the coat with the teeth pointing away from you and tilted slightly downward (*Photo 8-1*); then gently push the knife through the coat with a long firm stroke, working with the grain and following the contour of the dog (*Photo 8-2*). Do this regularly over the entire body area, but never over the furnishings, until the coat lays close and tight. A piece of hack saw blade is an ideal tool for carding a short coat. It has been well established that carding and rolling, coupled with oiling and brushing, will produce the most desirable coat and keep the jacket in excellent condition for the maximum period of time.

DAILY CARE

Once the dog starts coming into full coat, daily care becomes doubly important. After the routine preliminaries have been taken care of, spray a liberal amount of coat conditioner over the jacket and brush briskly for at least fifteen minutes with a hound glove or natural bristle brush. Special attention should be given to problem areas, such as the shoulders and hips. Most dogs enjoy this part of grooming and will brace contentedly against the pressure of the brush (*Photo 8-3*).

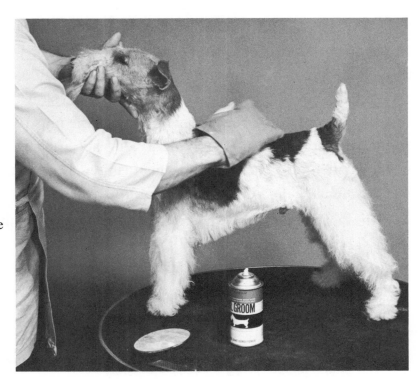

8-3. Hound Glove

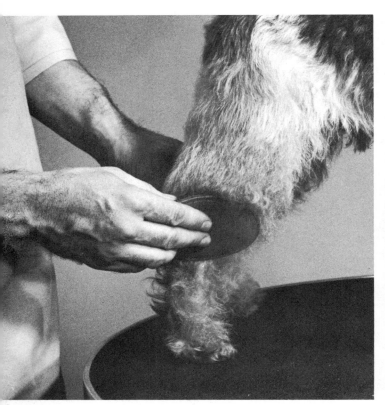 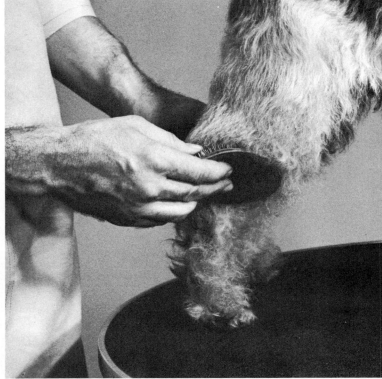

8-4. Pin Brushing   8-5. Massaging

CARE OF FURNISHINGS

Correct use of the "pin palm" not only serves to brush out the furnishings and remove unwanted dead hair, but also stimulates additional growth to help produce the dense furnishings that are so difficult to acquire.

Holding the edge of the pin brush with your fingers, press the pins into the furnishings (*Photo 8-4*). Rotate the pin palm lightly to massage the skin by describing small circles with your finger tips (*Photo 8-5*). Do this several times; then carefully peel away the palm with a slow downward motion. When this is done correctly, the hair will cling to the pins (*Photo 8-6*) and make the furnishings stand out, thus giving a very full appearance. Work over the furnishings, including the beard, in this fashion. If you find that you are removing too much hair, you should carefully review your technique.

If the furnishings become very wispy or flyaway, it may be necessary to tip them. This means trimming about quarter of an inch off the ends with a stripping knife once a month until the furnishings tighten up again.

CHALKING

As a rule terriers that are being shown should not be bathed. This is because excessive wetting loosens the hair and causes the coat to blow. In white dogs the problem of maintaining that sparkling white appearance is resolved by using white chalk as a cleaning agent. Colored chalk is also available for use on the other terrier breeds. Chalk also makes the furnishings easier to control and dries the oils out of the hair so that it achieves the desirable harsh texture. Chalk comes in both powdered form or in a block (*Photo 8-7*), and may be applied when the coat is either wet or dry. The general practice is to use powdered chalk on a wet coat and block chalk for dry applications or touch up work. As specified in Chapter 16, Section 9-B of the American Kennel Club's book entitled *Rules Applying to Registration and Dog Shows,* all traces of chalk must be removed from the coat before the dog enters the ring.

8-6. Hair Clinging to Pin Brush

8-7. Block Chalk

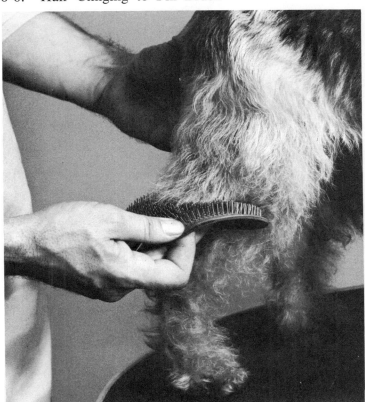
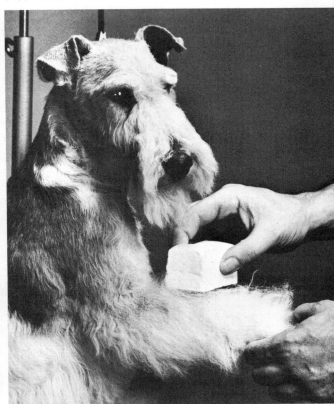

For wet application, the furnishings should be sponged down with a minimum amount of tepid water and pure liquid soap that will not soften the hair (*Photo 8-8*). The surface of the jacket should be sponged enough to dampen the coat. Dry the furnishings with a towel and apply a fine film of petroleum jelly over the entire dog by rubbing a small amount between the palms of your hands and then gently stroking the coat and furnishings. Apply a dusting of chalk to the legs, underchest, and beard with a bristle brush and work the chalk into the hair with a light, inward motion. On the body areas the chalk should be applied with the grain of the hair and special care should be taken to avoid over-powdering colored areas. The eyebrows can be chalked without undue fuss by taking a pinch of chalk between your fingers and applying it carefully while the dog's head is bent down.

8-8.   Sponging

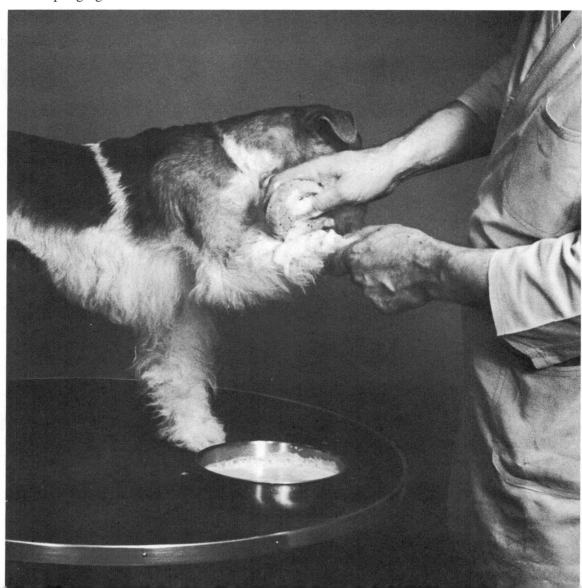

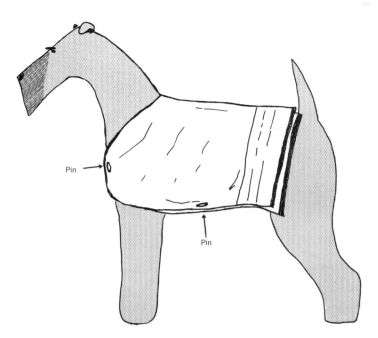

Pin

Pin

Diagram 17. Sacking

After the dog is chalked, he can be "sacked up" to flatten his coat (*Diagram 17*). This is accomplished by folding a bath towel in half, draping it over the dog's back, and pinning it in front of the chest and under the belly. Place the dog in a warm, confined area until he is completely dry. After this all the surplus powder must be brushed out, and, once again, a pure bristle brush is the most satisfactory for the purpose.

During chalking, dust can easily get into the dog's eyes. To remove irritating particles and to soothe the eyes after chalking and brushing have been completed, you can apply "Eye Brite" drops (*Photo* 8-9).

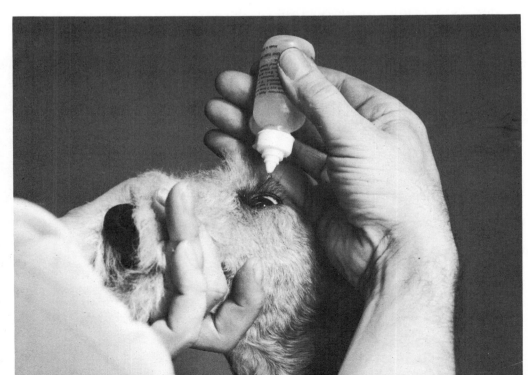

8-9. Eye Drops

67

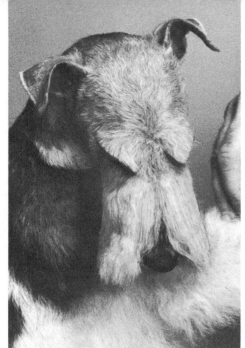

8-10.   Adding Length

FINAL PREPARATION FOR SHOW

The beard should be trimmed forward in such a fashion as to add length to the dog's head (*Photo 8-10*). For the best effect comb the eyebrows and beard forward in a single exaggerated movement (*Photo 8-11*).

To shape the eyebrows of the long-legged terriers, with the exception of the Schnauzer (*Photo 8-12*), comb the eyebrows forward, separate the brow at the center of the eye, and carefully pluck off the outer half of the brow (*Photo 8-13*). Comb the remainder of the eyebrow forward and trim diagonally with scissors (*Photo 8-14*); then pick the hair out at the stop to divide the eyebrows. For detailed instructions on trimming Schnauzer eyebrows, see page 38, under "Scissoring" in the section on pet grooming.

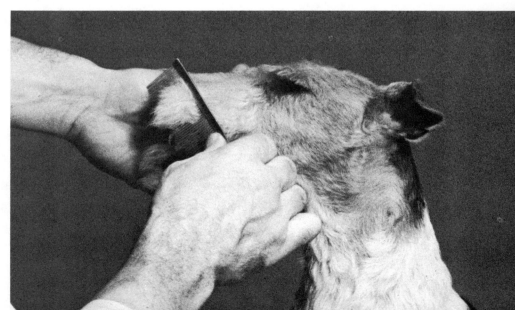

8-11.   Combing Eyebrows
and Beard

68

8-12.   Schnauzer—"Dark Victory"

8-13.   Plucking Outer Eyebrow

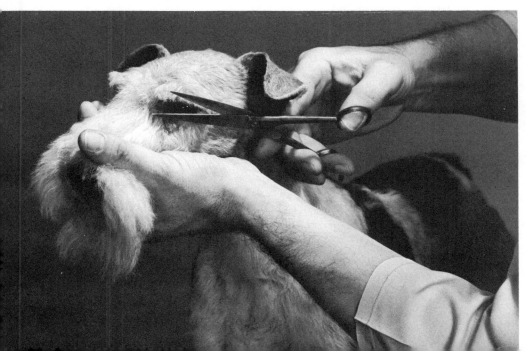

8-14.   Scissoring Eyebrows

69

8-15. Lakeland Terrier—"Stingray"

The Lakeland terrier does not have divided eyebrows but retains a fall between the eyes, which blends into the hair on the muzzle. The eyebrows are trimmed diagonally to expose the eye (*Photo 8-15 and also refer back to Diagram 8*). Some handlers choose to groom their Airedales in similar fashion, but this is more or less optional and principally a matter of taste.

The hair on the underchest must be shaped and trimmed in a gently inclining line from the elbow to the thigh. Trim around the tenders with the scissors (*Photo 8-17*) until you become proficient enough to do this with a stripping knife.

Clip the underbelly with a No. 10 blade as is described in detail on page 35. Clean out the pads as described on page 46. Trim around the feet with the scissors (*Photo 8-18*).

Continue working the coat and furnishings until everything blends in, and, hopefully, you will soon have your terrier looking like a show champion (*Photo 8-19 and Diagram 18*).

8-16. Airedale

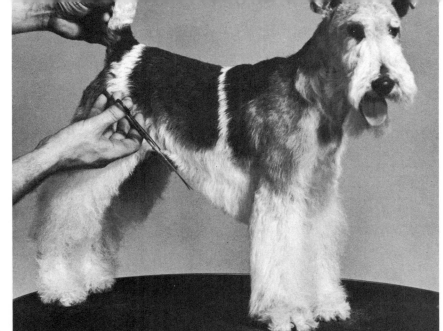

8-17. Scissoring Tenders

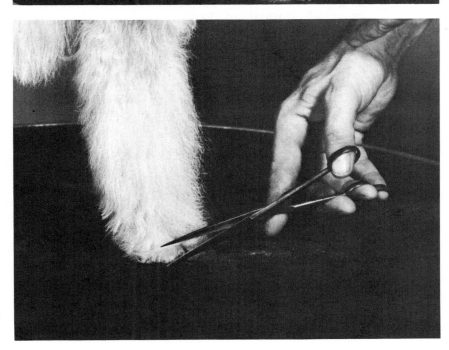

8-18. Scissoring
Around Feet

Diagram 18. Terrier in Full Coat   8-19. Show Dog Look

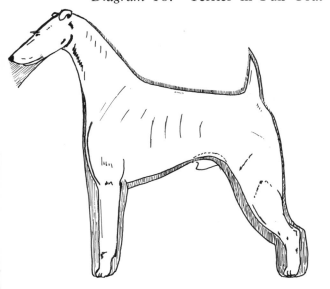

CHAPTER 9

THE SHORT-LEGGED TERRIERS

SCOTTISH TERRIER   WEST HIGHLAND WHITE   SEALYHAM

One of the most important points to remember when stripping a Scottie, Sealy, or Westie is the necessity of retaining that squat, solid appearance. Careful attention must be given to the distinctive features that characterize these breeds: note the full beard, overhanging eyebrows, and tufted ears of the Scottie (*Photo 9-1*); the full face and heavy, undivided eyebrows of the Sealy (*Photo 9-2*); and the full head without eyebrow definition of the Westie (*Photo 9-3*). In addition, these terriers retain a natural, skirted appearance and, thus, their legs and underparts do not normally need to be shaped or fashioned. As these breeds do not require staggered stripping, the entire job can be completed in one session.

The area to be stripped extends from the head to the tail; over the backs and sides to the point of the shoulder, which is midway between the withers and the elbow; and rearward to the stern.

SCOTTISH TERRIER

The way a Scottie's ears are trimmed makes a unique contribution to its expression. A pompon of hair is left attached to the head and to the front inner edge of the ear. To produce this effect you should strip the back of the ears first, then strip the front, doing the outer edge and only the upper half of the inside edge. Scissor carefully around the ear but only midway down on the inside. To get the pompon the right length for the ear, fold half of the ear down

9-1.   Sealyham—"Alcide"

9-2.   Scottish Terrier—"Grenadier"

9-3.   West Highland White—
"Weaver's Drummond"

73

cut the surplus hair in a straight line, level with the folded edge. Repeat for the opposite ear.

The beard should be left full, and this is achieved by scissoring it straight from the outer corner of the eyebrow to the corner of the mouth. The eyebrows should also be left full so that they resemble a shade or visor extending diagonally from the outer corners to the inner edges of the eyes and divided at the stop to form two right angle triangles with the perpendicular lines parallel on the inside. For greater detail on shaping Scottie eyebrows, read page 38, of the section on pet grooming. The head should be kept medium short, the neck clean.

SEALYHAM

The Sealy head should be very full. The eyebrows should be left undivided, but they can either be trimmed to give a visor-like effect or left with a fall in the center of the brow to blend into the hair on the muzzle, and they should be scissored diagonally to expose the eyes. The underbeard is also left very full

9-4.   Cairn Terrier—"Caithness Colonel"

and this, coupled with the heavy brow, creates a rounded effect. The top of the head, the ears, and throat should all be trimmed close.

WEST HIGHLAND WHITE

The Westie head is never stripped; any tidying that may be necessary is done with a stripping knife. The head should be shaped so that it looks completely round when seen from the front and resembles two soup plates, one inverted on top of the other, when seen from the side. The upper half of the ears should be picked off and the lower half of the outer edges trimmed so as not to interfere with the shape of the face. The throat should be trimmed close.

OTHER TERRIER BREEDS

The remainder of the short-legged terriers, such as the Cairn and the Norwich, can be trimmed like the Westie, except that their ears should be stripped to the base (*Photos 9-4 and 9-5*).

9-5.   Norwich Terrier—"Noel's Eve"

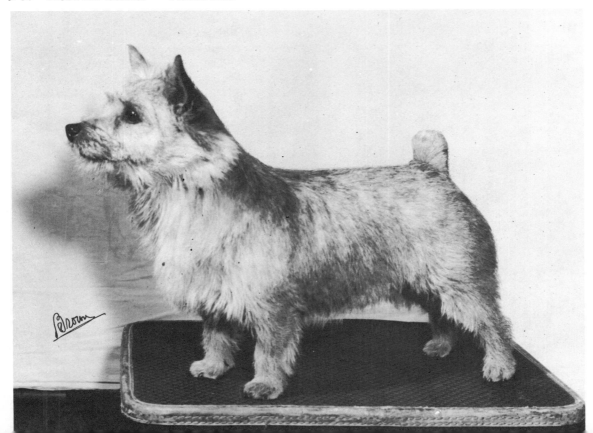

CHAPTER 10

TOPPING OFF THE COAT

If your dog has already come into coat, or if, for some reason, the coat has gotten ahead of you, you may still be able to save it or, at least, hold it long enough to make a number of shows by topping off the jacket. Plucking the hair out with the fingers, rather than with a stripping knife, will usually produce the best results in these cases because more control can be exercised over the amount of coat that is being removed. "Hold-Tite Spray Grip," or any similar non-slip product obtainable from most sporting goods stores, can be applied to your fingers to make the task easier. Ruff the coat as you would when using the stripper but, instead of trapping the hair between your thumb and the knife, trap it between your thumb and forefinger and pluck it out with the grain in the normal fashion (*Photo 10-1*). Work over the coat in this way about twice a week, removing only the worst of the top coat. Next, card

10-1.   Plucking

10-2.   Stripping Throat

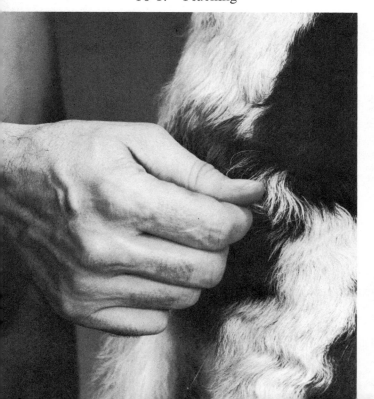
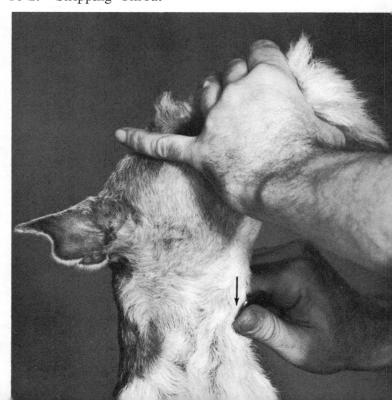

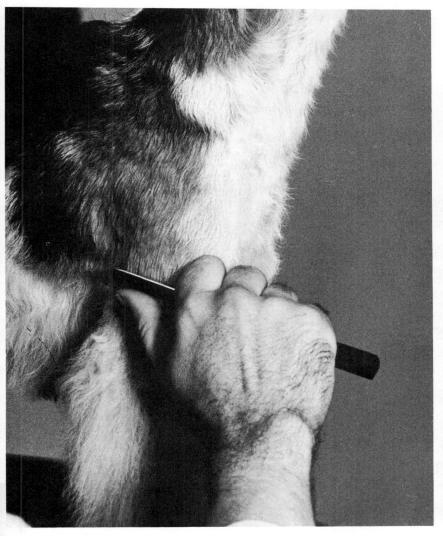

10-3. Blending Shoulders and Legs

10-4. Correct   Incorrect

the undercoat as previously described until the coat lays flat. Strip the throat and front close with a fine stripping knife (*Photo 10-2*).

The shoulders must also be cleaned off and blended evenly with the leg furnishings (*Photo 10-3*) to avoid harsh lines and unsightly undulations. Photo 10-4 indicates the right and wrong ways of dealing with the front legs.

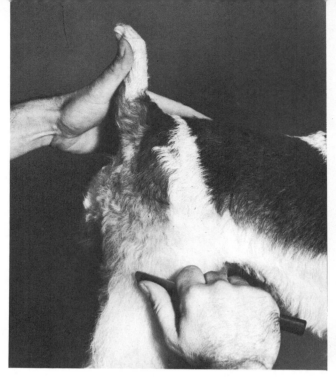

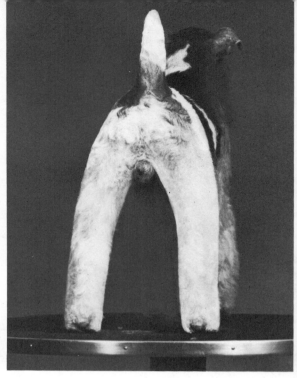

10-5. Blending Hindquarters

10-6. Rear Legs Arch-Like

The hindquarters must also be blended (*Photo 10-5*) so that there are no noticeable definitions from the top of the hips, down the thighs, past the hocks, and to the feet. The inside, as well as the outside, of the rear legs should be shaped to resemble an arch (*Photo 10-6*).

The head must be trimmed close in order to present clean lines. For this reason the top and sides of the head (*Photo 10-7*), the ears, and the throat must be worked on regularly.

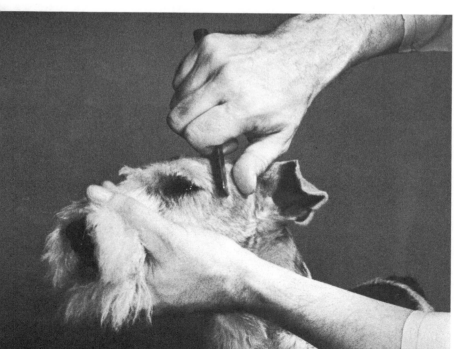

10-7. Trimming Head

CHAPTER 11

MISCELLANEOUS AND FINE POINTS

Learning the basic skills is not enough for the terrier fancier who wants to do a professional-looking job. Mastering the fine points of the art of dog grooming is also essential. Did you neglect to pluck his ears or trim his nails? Is he completely clean? Have you avoided all clipper burns and rashes? Very often it is these extra little attentions that distinguish the good groomer from the mediocre one. If the groomer happens to be a professional, his knowledge of these small but important matters will help cement the relationship between his customers and himself. Many terrier owners will travel far out of their way to patronize a favorite groomer.

USE OF SCISSORS

Scissoring properly is an art in itself. It will take a great deal of experience before you are able to do it right. To scissor quickly and comfortably, hold the shears firmly (*Photo 11-1*) with your little finger hooked over the open shank, the tip of your third finger through the finger hold, and your second finger resting on the handle. Your index finger is used to brace the scissors, and the tip of your thumb goes into the thumb hole. Cut by holding the lower section of the shears as still as possible and working mainly with your thumb.

11-1. Proper Scissoring

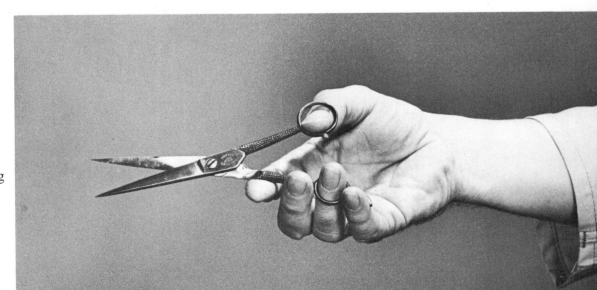

NAIL TRIMMING

City dogs are generally house pets, and, in the high-storied apartments where they make their homes, they seldom get enough exercise. Consequently, their nails do not receive the natural grinding which comes with a reasonable amount of outdoor activity, and they have to be trimmed regularly.

The thing to be concerned about here is the quick under the nail. The novice should be content to trim just the tips at first. This is done by holding the paw firmly and trimming with short, decisive strokes (*Photo 11-2*). Be sure to check the dog for dewclaws.

When you become familiar with this operation, you will know exactly how high up on the nail you can go without causing bleeding. But until you do, it is wise to play it safe, and if bleeding should occur, have a can of ferric subsulfate or Monsell solution on hand. This stops the flow of blood immediately. These medications are available at most drugstores in both powder and liquid form.

The best time to trim the dog's nails is just before his bath; the worst time, as many groomers have discovered to their sorrow, is at the end of the grooming job when the dog is beautifully turned out. If the nails are trimmed at this point and bleeding occurs, the coat may become smeared and the job is ruined.

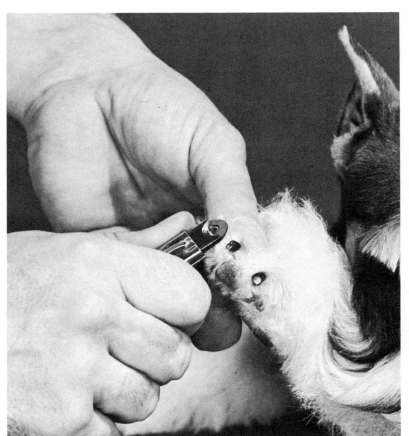

11-2. Nail Trimming

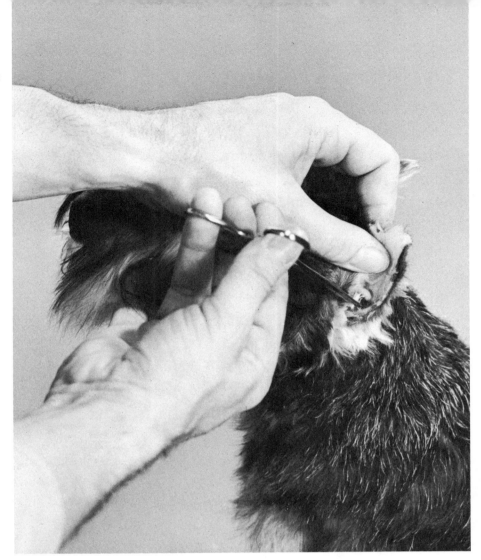

EAR PLUCKING

Purchase a can of ear powder from your pet dealer before you begin to clean your dog's ears. Shake a little of it into the ear and spread it through the hairs. This will cause the hairs to become dry and brittle so that they are easier to pull out. Use your fingers in the beginning; later, when you are more experienced, a pair of hemostats or ear pluckers may be used *(Photo 11-3)*. Pluck the hairs with a quick rolling motion—the entire job should take only a few minutes.

The best time to clean the dog's ears is before his bath, at the same time that you trim his nails, so that any trace of liquid or powder left on the coat will be washed away.

Never attempt to treat the dog's ears if they are infected. This is a matter for the veterinarian.

CLIPPER BURNS AND RASHES

Many pet owners say that their dogs come back from grooming salons with clipper burns and rashes. These owners often claim that the dog did not have anything like that before going to the grooming shop and that their veterinarians diagnosed the mark as a clipper burn. Occasionally this may be true— there are, of course, times when the grooming salon is at fault. As a rule, however, this will not happen at a reputable grooming salon where quality comes first. Dogs, like people, vary in skin sensitivity. Some have very tender skins and show such marks after a close clipping. When a clipper burn does develop in spite of the best precautions, you can apply any one of a half-dozen soothing lotions specially prepared for dogs. In addition, try not to clip the sensitive spots as close the next time.

Clipper burns may also develop if the clippers are allowed to run so long that the blades get too hot. To avoid this the groomer must feel the blade occasionally during the clipping. A hot blade can be instantly cooled, lubricated, and sanitized with hair clipper spray. Before this product came on the market, the process took much longer. It was necessary to change the blades frequently or to stop and wait until the blade cooled down.

Clipping the dog before his bath is another cause of clipper rash. As the reader will recall, at the beginning of this book the necessity of thoroughly brushing and bathing the dog before clipping was well stressed. The alternative can lead to discomfort and, perhaps, infection from the combination of hot clippers and dirty skin. It is also much easier to clip a clean dog.

If, despite all precautions, the dog's skin still becomes irritated, have him checked by a veterinarian.

FLEA BATH

Fleas are not only a discomfort to your dog, but also a major cause of worm infections which can be dangerous to his health. Don't waste any time in combating fleas once they appear. There are several good insecticide shampoos on the market that are easy to apply; so, instead of using a regular shampoo for bathing, use a flea shampoo.

WORMING

The health of your dog is an important part of his pre-show preparation. A well-conditioned dog will always look the part, and a dull, listless specimen will not impress the judges regardless of how carefully groomed he may be. Conditioning must start from the inside, and the first step is to insure that your dog is free of internal parasites. This is another job for your vet. Many new dog owners do not realize that the most debilitating types of worms are not readily visible to the naked eye and that a microscopic examination of the dog's stool is the only reliable method of determining the presence of worms.

FEEDING AND EXERCISE

"We are what we eat." Whoever made that observation had the right idea, and dogs, as well as people, need a well balanced diet. The best thing to feed your dog is dog food—not food for human diet. People who, in a misguided act of kindness, add table scraps to commercial dog food to make it more palatable may find that their dogs will eventually refuse to eat dog food altogether. Such dogs may become very "picky" and, consequently, get into poor condition.

Dry, flaky skin or a dull coat, excessive shedding, itching, and scratching without evidence of parasites, may be a symptom of fatty acid deficiency. A few drops of Lambert-Kay's "Linatone" added to a balanced diet may help to curb this condition and enhance the beauty and luster of the coat.

Controlled exercise in the form of daily road work is undoubtedly the best form of conditioning exercise for any breed of dog. Walking will rapidly improve muscle tone, tighten up the feet, and wear down the nails. If possible, walk your dog several miles every day. That *you*, too, will look and feel fitter, may be a little extra bonus.

WHAT IS A SHOW DOG?

Being American Kennel Club registered is only part of the requirement for a show dog. The dog must also qualify as a representative of its breed by conforming to the AKC standard set up for that breed. Included in the standard are specifications which, if not complied with, incur mandatory disqualification from AKC competition. For example, a miniature Schnauzer that is over four-teen inches at the withers, is solid white in color, or has white patches on his body is ineligible for competition. All male dogs that are monorchid or cryptor-chid are automatically barred. So are Wire Fox terriers with pricked ears. Be sure you find out as much as you can about the requirements of your particular fancy before you buy a puppy. You may write to the American Kennel Club, 51 Madison Ave., New York, New York 10016, for a copy of the standard for any recognized breed.

All dog show entries must be recorded on official entry forms. These may be obtained by writing to the superintendent of a particular show.. A list of show superintendents is included in every issue of *Pure-Bred Dogs American Kennel Club Gazette,* a monthly magazine published by the AKC. The entry forms are self-explanatory.

BUYING A PUPPY

If you are interested in buying a puppy, go to a reputable breeder—that is, a person who has established a reputation for breeding and selling quality dogs. It will be cheaper in the long run, even if the puppy initially costs more than it would from some backyard breeder. In addition, it is important that the dog come from the type of breeder who will accustom him to being groomed and handled as soon as he is old enough. This will greatly reduce the chores of the new puppy owner who decides to do everything himself.

How often have we heard the lament, "We were promised papers, but we never got them." Make sure you either get the AKC Registration Forms from the breeder as soon as you buy the puppy or else suggest withholding a frac-tion on the payment until such time as the papers are made over to you. After all, if you buy an AKC registered puppy and never receive the registration papers, you have actually been given only a part of your purchase.

Have your puppy checked by a veterinarian *immediately* and make sure that the dog has had all its shots before you expose him to the outside world. The vet is your pet's doctor—always consult him if you are concerned about your puppy's health.

LIKE YOUR WORK

Taking care of a dog and grooming it is no lazy man's paradise, but not all of the work is unpleasant or overly difficult. Many dog owners became professionals simply because they were so fond of animals, and several of these men and women now hold top positions in the dog world.

Whether done by a professional or amateur, expert or beginner, the grooming process should be a pleasure, not an ordeal, for both dog and groomer. The ideal relationship is one where the dog looks forward to being groomed. What a happy advertisement it is for the professional when a patron's dog comes in wagging his tail instead of tugging at his leash! The whole process is easier when the dog is not balky or frightened, and the groomer can then do a more careful job.

CHAPTER 12

THE DOG GROOMING SALON

This section is devoted to those who wish to go beyond trimming their own dog or dogs and turn this hobby into a profitable career. Proper schooling, while not yet required by law in many states is, of course, necessary. If you decide to turn professional, attend a licensed school and take an advanced course. In the long run, it will be the most worthwhile part of your investment.

Dog-grooming salons are flourishing throughout the country, and, in the past few years, they have become an industry in themselves. Indeed, pets—breeding them, caring for them, and grooming them—have become big business.

While the poodle is indisputably the leading single breed in the country and is largely responsible for the healthy condition of the dog-grooming business, the combined terrier breeds run the poodle a close second. Moreover, the fact that the pet terrier can be clipped in half the time that it takes to clip the poodle makes them far more profitable to deal with. Indeed, there is a certain trend, especially in the larger cities, toward dog-grooming shops that specialize exclusively in terriers. The Schnauzer in particular has assumed a commanding lead in terrier registrations.

A dog grooming career is so attractive to many people because it permits you to combine both avocation and vocation; to establish a profitable business out of something you like to do; it is a growing and profitable field; and the initial investment is very low.

A major part of the investment will go into equipment. A professional groomer requires professional tools. The following equipment is absolutely essential:

Cages, preferably of galvanized metal or steel (*Photo 12-1*).

Cage dryer for drying (*Photo 12-1*).

Bathtub—can be a used model but must stand or be elevated to a waist-high position (*Photo 12-2*).

12-1. Cage Unit of Four
with Cage Dryers

12-2. Bathtub, Waist-High

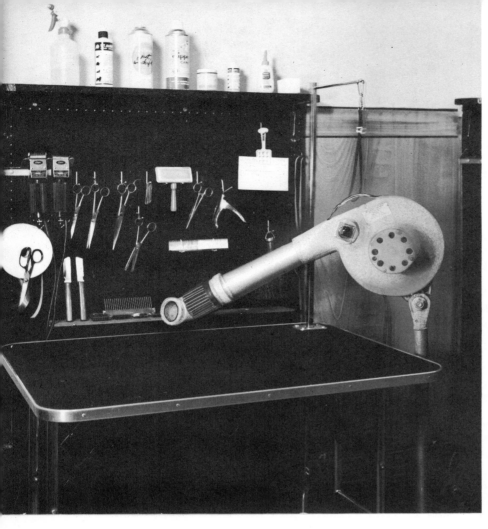

12-3. Professional Work Area

Floor dryer for fluffing (*Photo 12-3*).

Grooming table with post and loop (*Photo 12-3*).

Clippers, blades, shampoos, brushes, combs, nail trimmers, scissors, ear powders, ear plucker, etc. (*Photo 12-3*), as well as all the necessary cleaning equipment.

A good vacuum cleaner — we recommend an "Industrial Shop Vacuum," which can be purchased at major department stores.

LOCATION

Of course, the field can be quite competitive, and selecting a location for your salon is as important in dog grooming as in any other business. Where the field is already crowded and there are many established salons, it may be difficult for the newcomer to survive. There are still many areas where no shops exist or competition is negligible and trade available, and a professional who takes pride in his work and is not exorbitant in his fees has nothing to fear. However, the question of location is important enough to warrant special attention. To put it more sharply, good grooming alone is not enough for success —location is almost equally important. Good grooming plus good location equal success.

Unfortunately, too many good groomers become so enamored with their own ability that they think all they have to do is set up a shop almost anywhere in town and people will flock to them. This is not so, especially where already established shops present keen competition. The good groomer will then die a slow death.

For the inexperienced grooming shop owner, location is doubly important. The new shop owner who is so foolish as to locate in any hole in the wall in a slum area, will find himself faced with a quick, but not a painless, death. When we are asked if a new shop can afford to pay the high rents of the big cities today, we can only answer with another question: "Can you afford to go into business at all?" Every business requires an investment, which includes rent; and again we repeat that dog grooming requires less of an investment than almost any other business we know, including the corner candy store.

In general, then, we can answer the question of how much rent to pay by saying that it is far better to pay a higher rent in a good area—the returns will more than compensate for this percentage of your overhead.

To sum up the question of location, we can do no better than to suggest that you conduct a diligent search for a shop in a good area, that you resign yourself to paying rents comparable to those paid by other good stores.

SETTING UP A SHOP

The three things necessary for the new dog-grooming salon are, in order of importance, quality grooming, a desirable location, and a well organized and attractive shop.

The first factor, "quality grooming," is what this book is all about. The second factor, "location," is discussed above. The third factor requires more elaboration.

Every effort should be made to make the shop's decor as bright as possible since good light aids grooming efficiency. For example, the walls should be painted a light color to brighten the grooming area, and the lighting fixtures should be selected on the basis of how much light they cast as well as on their appearance. Of course, strong daylight provides ideal lighting, but there is never enough, particularly during winter when darkness comes early and many days are overcast.

Probably the most expensive single item that you will have to buy for your shop will be the cages. Each dog that comes into your shop should have a separate cage. These cages come in units of two, four, six, or eight; or single units can be custom-made. The best cages are made of galvanized metal or steel and are equipped with sliding pans for easy cleaning. Prices vary, depending on quality and make. A unit of four will usually cost about $200.

Your next most expensive purchase will be the floor dryer used to fluff dry the dog. These dryers run anywhere between $120 and $160, and most shops need two or more. Cage dryers cost between $50 and $60. You will also need grooming tables, which come complete with a grooming post and cost about $40 each. You can count on spending around $300 for clippers, blades, scissors, combs, brushes, shampoos, nail trimmers, and other minor items.

Roughly, then, the entire cost of the essential items will be between $700 and $800. Since it is wise to have at least double of everything, plan to spend about $1,500. When you add the cost of rent, fixtures, and furnishings, to this total, you can think realistically of opening a shop with a minimum capital of $3,000. Of course, you will need a reserve until the business is on a sound basis. Still, even if the investment totals somewhere between $3,500 and $4,000, there are almost no other businesses in which an individual can reap substantial returns within a year's time on such a low original investment.

Cleanliness is a necessity in a dog-grooming shop. You cannot overdo the cleaning, disinfecting, and sanitizing. The first impression you make on a customer should be your best one, and a spotless shop is half the battle. This means a well-kept workroom, as well as an attractive reception room. The days of the "pet shop look," with foul odors and littered floors, are gone forever.

Another "must" is insurance. You will need a property damage and public liability policy, a fire and theft policy, and a plate glass policy. They all have low annual premiums.

Before you set your fees, learn the prevailing price scale in the salon's immediate and surrounding area; then charge accordingly. Do not overcharge for a service or start out with cut-rate prices in the hope of enticing customers away from a nearby competitor. You will find it extremely difficult to raise your prices later.

It is also wise to persuade your customers of the desirability of coming in regularly to have their dogs groomed. Add an extra charge if the customers have allowed too much time to elapse between groomings, and charge extra if a dog has been neglected and comes in badly matted so that it requires considerable extra time to brush him. Flea baths may also warrant an extra fee. Such charges should not be exorbitant, but, if properly set, they may help teach the owner to keep his dog in better condition.

Hang diagrams or photographs of the various clips and breeds on your wall. Be sure they are in a prominent spot so that the customer can point to one and say, "That's what I want." This saves a lot of confusion and aggravation. Also, have your scale of prices prominently displayed so that there is no mix-up or embarrassment regarding any of your fees.

Some advertising is essential. Get as much good publicity as you can, and always remember that the best recommendation is a satisfied customer. It is also a good idea to sell some accessories, such as brushes, combs, collars, leashes, coats, shampoos, and deodorants. This will be convenient for your customers and, of course, will supplement your income.

Naturally, we cannot cover every possible situation which may arise in a dog-grooming shop. Common sense and experience must prevail. However, here are a few tips which may help along the way:

Do not groom problem dogs.

Dogs should come in at a certain hour in the morning and be picked up at a stated time in the evening.

Take extra precautions to insure the safety of the dogs — for example, open doors are an open invitation to run out.

Keep precise file cards on every dog.

Make it a practice to accept only as many dogs as you have time to groom well.

CHAPTER 13

SOFT-COATED TERRIERS

Paradoxically, grooming soft-coated terriers like the Kerry blue and the Bedlington is more like poodle grooming than terrier grooming. These terriers are not stripped or plucked. We would suggest that if you have a Kerry or Bedlington you should familiarize yourself with the brushing, bathing, drying and scissoring techniques described in our book "Clipping And Grooming Your Poodle," since space does not permit such detailed instructions here. If the poodle book is not readily available, study the fundamentals described in Chapters 1 and 2 of this book.

KERRY BLUE

Clipping on the Head

The area to be clipped on the head is quite small, illustrated by light shading on Diagram 19. Use a No. 10 blade, working with the grain. Start at a point one-half inch behind the outer corner of the eye and clip straight back to the inner corner of the ear. Clip around the back of the ear to the lower edge of the base, leaving a clearly defined line between the ear and the side of the head; do this on both sides. Then, clip a diagonal line to a point approximately 2 inches below the Adam's apple; this will form a deep V when the proce-

92

Front   Rear

Diagram 19.   Kerry Blue

dure is repeated on the opposite side. *Do not* clip the foreskull. This area will be scissored. Clip the ears clean both front and back by laying the flap of the ear flat on the palm of the hand and clipping with the grain. Trim closely around the edges with scissors.

Trimming the Kerry consists mostly of scissor work. For the best effect the Kerry should be scissored with the grain of the hair. Lift the ends of the coat with the tip of the comb and allow the hair to fall. Scissor off the hair that does not fall naturally into place. Repeat this procedure over the entire dog until you have achieved the desired effect. Encourage the dog to shake from time to time; remove any loose ends that may appear. Scissoring is done systematically in the following order: Head; Neck; Front and Shoulders; Body; Rear; and Tail.

Head

Comb the hair on the face forward including the beard and eyebrows. Scissor the hair on the foreskull as short as possible. Lay the scissors flat along the skull pointing forward, taking care to use the center of the blades and not the tips, as cutting with the tips tends to gouge the coat. The length of the hair should increase slightly towards the back skull. Next, gently taper the area on Diagram 19 from the very short clipped area to blend evenly into the beard. Clean off surplus under beard to extend the length of head. Remove excess hair from under the chin so that the head does not look coarse or bulky.

The Kerry Blue retains a fall of hair in the center of the brow, also referred to as bangs, which should blend smoothly with the hair on the foreface. Scissor surplus hair from above the eyebrows and trim the outer edges diagonally towards the center, exposing about one third of the eye.

Neck, Front, and Shoulders

Scissor the front of the neck to look straight and clean. The length of the hair should increase gently from the clipped area down the throat and neck to the chest in an unbroken line, blending with the shoulders, and on into the front furnishings. The neck should be slightly arched; trim the hair on the back of the neck starting short at the back of the skull, gradually increasing in length to about one to one-and-a-half inches at the withers, sufficiently long enough to blend cleanly with the shoulders, which is scissored close enough to be elegant without losing strength.

Body

The length of the body coat should vary gradually from approximately one inch on the back to about one-and-one-half inches at the sides and quarters giving a solid and formidable appearance. Scissor the back flat leaving the hair a little less than 1 inch long, lengthening at the sides to give a moderately barrel-like spring of rib, tapering slightly towards the underchest which should be nicely rounded off. Tuckup should be moderate.

Rear

The rear quarters are shaped to look powerful but not bulky, the legs scissored to show good angulation, and well let-down hocks.

Tail

Trim the tail close at the back and about half an inch long on the remaining sides, slightly larger at the base, tapering to a blunt tip. The finished product should demonstrate a combination of power and elegance.

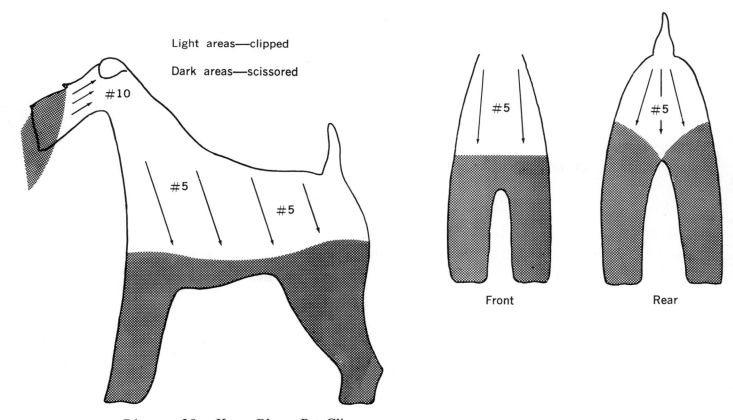

Diagram 20. Kerry Blue—Pet Clip

Legs

The front legs must be scissored to look as round and straight as possible. To do this, comb the hair out from the leg and then shake the leg gently as if you were "shaking hands," trim off all protruding ends. Repeat this procedure until the hair falls neatly into place each time you shake the leg. To keep the dog standing still as you scissor, lift the leg opposite the one that you are working on, causing the dog to keep its weight on the leg you are scissoring. Keep the shears parallel with the leg at all times, cut either up or down but never across. The rear legs must be trimmed to follow the sweep of the stifle, closer at the back and on the insides, to demonstrate good angulation and well let-down hocks.

Pet Clip

The Kerry owner who does not intend to show his dog (and who wishes to save much of the time that would otherwise be spent on scissoring) may clip the entire body area with a No. 5 blade (*Diagram 20*). For the rest, the scissoring technique remains essentially the same but there is much less of it.

BEDLINGTON

The Bedlington must be brushed, combed, bathed, and fluff-dried—very much like the poodle. Follow the step-by-step procedures as outlined in Chapters 1 and 2, if the Poodle book is not available.

Fluff Drying

The secret of the "powder puff" look on the Bedlington is in the fluff drying process. Fluff drying is a combination of brushing and drying with a blower. Hot air is directed at the area being brushed. A good dryer for this purpose is the one mentioned in the equipment section, the Oster airjet dryer. (It can also be used in milady's boudoir if purchased with a hood.) Brush drying or fluff drying must be done like every other step, systematically and methodically, starting with the legs and moving on to the body, tail, head, and ears. Use light strokes, fluffing the dog's coat as the blowing process separates the hairs. Those who wish to do their fluff drying more professionally will, of course, use the standard floor dryer. Then quickly comb out the entire coat. When this is finished, rest the dog, and incidentally, yourself.

Actually, the brushing, bathing, and fluff drying processes are considered the tedious parts of grooming by some, although many pet lovers do not seem to mind this work in the least. When one becomes adept in these techniques, the processes become simpler and go faster.

Clipping the Head

Using a No. 10 or No. 15 blade either with or against the grain (depending on the degree of closeness desired), clip the head from the corner of the mouth to the outer corner of the eye. From the corner of the eye back to the inner corner of the ear, clip around the back of the ear to the lower edge of the base, leaving a clearly defined line between the ear and the side of the head. Repeat on both sides. From the base of the ear clip a diagonal line to a point approximately 2 inches below the Adam's apple. This will form a deep V when the procedure is repeated on the opposite side. Clip the underjaw clean. *Do not* clip any other part of the head, except the ears.

Ears

Clip ears back and front with a No. 10 or No. 15 blade by laying the flap of the ear flat on the palm of the hand, leave a diamond shaped tassel, about 1½ to 2 inches long at the end (*Diagram 21*). Scissor around the edges of the clipped portion.

Tail

With a No. 10 or No. 15 blade clip the length of the underpart of the tail from the base to the tip. Clip two thirds of the upper part of the tail for a rat-tail effect. Scissor the remaining one third to blend with the body (*Diagram 21*).

Scissoring

The Bedlington, like the Kerry Blue, requires mostly scissor work. Before starting to scissor the Bedlington, comb out the hair away from the body so that it literally stands on end. Scissor with a semicircular sweeping motion, keeping the elbow rigid and the wrist flexible. Use the closed shears to return the hair to the desired upright position after every six or eight cutting strokes.

Neck, Front & Shoulders

Scissor the front of the neck to look clean and straight, blending smoothly from clipped area to the chest. Trim the back of the neck with a slight arch, starting short at the base of the skull and gradually increasing in length to a maximum of

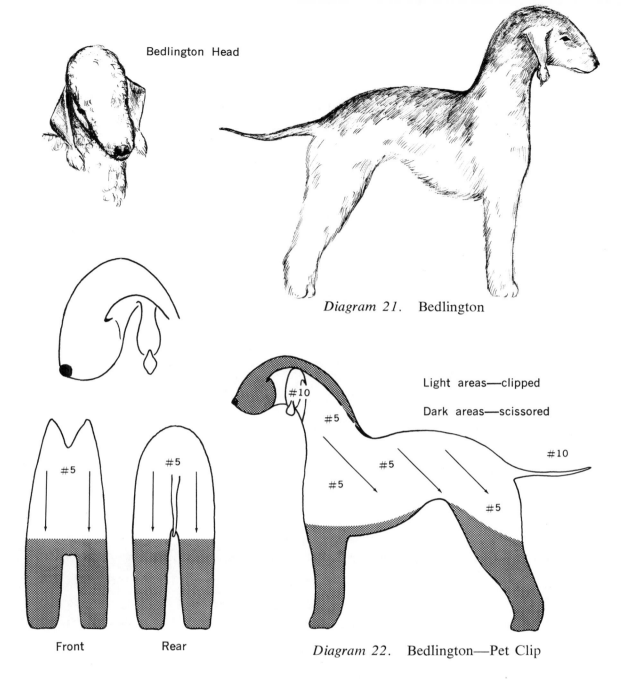

Bedlington Head

Diagram 21. Bedlington

Light areas—clipped

Dark areas—scissored

#10

#5

#5

#5

#5

#5

#10

#5

Front

Rear

Diagram 22. Bedlington—Pet Clip

1 inch so that the neck blends cleanly into the shoulder (which should be trimmed) to blend with the leg furnishings. When seen from the front, the dog should have a narrow appearance.

Body

Trim the back slightly less than an inch, shorter at the withers and along the sides. The Bedlington should always look flat-sided. The important feature is the profile—not so much the front or rear view. The chest should be left deep and wedge-shaped. Tuckup exaggerated.

Rear

The rear must be nicely shaped and angular, the hocks well down. Scissor feet round.

Topknot

The topknot must be scissored, blending with the neck at the occiput and curving forward gently to the nose, to give a distinct down-face effect. Must be very flat and clean at the sides—short enough not to be floppy, and about one inch or so high depending on texture. The sides of the face must be scissored to blend cleanly with the topknot.

Legs

Follow the same directions as given for the Kerry Blue.

The finished product should resemble a lamb. Diagram 21 is a good illustration of how it should look.

Pet Clip

For a pet clip use No. 5 blade on the body before scissoring the other parts (*Diagram 22*).

DANDIE DINMONT

The Dandie should be stripped in two sessions about three weeks apart, although it *can* be done all at once. The initial area should extend backwards from behind the shoulder to the tail, including about half the upper part of the tail, along the loin and flanks to the point of the rump, and down the sides to where the growth of the hair changes direction, not quite to the tenders.

The second area extends from the base of the skull down the neck and along the back to join the part already stripped. The sides of the neck and the shoulders are taken down almost to the elbow and back to blend into the previously stripped area.

The dead top coat should be carefully "pulled" as described in Chapter 10 without removing the undercoat. The apron is left full as is the hair on the underchest. The tuckup is scissored to accentuate the depth of chest. The head is left full, the topknot high and fluffy and shaped round. The hair around the eyes is carefully picked off to make the eyes look very large and round. The feet

Dandie Head

Diagram 23.   Dandie Dinmont

Front   Rear

Diagram 24.   Dandie Dinmont—Pet Clip

should be scissored round. The hair is kept close at the shoulders to accentuate the dip at the withers. As the dog comes into coat, systematic removal of surplus or dead hair—by picking and rolling—will maintain a good coat for an indefinite period.

Finally, the upper part of the muzzle must be clipped from below the eyes using a No. 10 blade. The ears are also clipped, leaving an ample tassel 2 inches from the tip as illustrated in Diagram 23. The edges of the clipped area on ears are neatly scissored.

Pet Clip

For Pet Clip use No. 7 blade on body areas that would otherwise be stripped (*Diagram 24*).

CHAPTER 14

CONCLUSION

Regardless of whether you are interested merely in learning to groom your own pet or in turning your hobby into a profitable business, your primary goal should be to do the best possible job of grooming the dog.

Our advice to those who feel unsure about their ability to handle dogs professionally is, "Take your time!" Before you invest in a shop of your own, go to a licensed school and get the necessary instruction. If you want to be a professional, learn how to groom all breeds.

Read as much theory as you can and acquaint yourself with the different breeds and their histories. Whether you are an individual terrier owner or a professional groomer, the more you know about these dogs, the better off you'll be. It's amazing how many questions you'll be asked about your own dog or the terrier with which you work.

How do you tell a good puppy from a poor one? What color is the best? How often should a bitch be mated? Where do we find a good stud? The answers to these questions and many more can be found in any comprehensive book on dogs.

Never attempt to act as a substitute veterinarian. A badly infected ear, a peculiar body growth, impacted anal glands, or any of the hundreds of other problems to which the dog is heir can be treated properly only by the man who has been trained to treat them.

On the other hand, some questions can be answered simply by reading and study. If someone asks a question and you don't know the answer, say so; if you do, be as helpful, clear, and specific as possible. Don't use confusing big terms. If you are a professional, your good advice can help you gain the confidence of your customer and, thus, will benefit you, too.

Your own dog, too, can be a walking advertisement for you. An improperly cared for, uncomfortable-looking, unkempt, or over-pampered dog will never win you any friends or customers. On the other hand, an elegant beauty, striding gracefully alongside his master, is the most eloquent testimonial to you as the owner, handler, and groomer.

GLOSSARY OF TERMS

AKC —— American Kennel Club.

BLOOM —— Coat in ideal condition.

BLOWN —— A dead coat—usually refers to a coat which is ready for stripping.

BREED STANDARD —— The official specifications for each breed as drawn up by the parent breed club, e.g., "The Miniature Schnauzer Club of America," and approved by the AKC, as representing the ideal.

CARDING —— Combing or raking through the coat to remove excess undercoat.

CLEAN —— Smooth, straight lines.

CONFORMATION —— How the physical structure of a dog corresponds to the official AKC standard for that breed.

JACKET —— Tight body coat of a terrier in full bloom.

PLUCKING —— Pulling out the coat with the first two fingers and thumb.

ROLLING —— Grasping the ends of the hair between the first two fingers and thumb and snapping the fingers to force the hair to roll between the fingers and thumb; thus removing dead or unwanted hair.

SACKING —— Wrapping dog in a large towel in order to flatten the coat.

SHOW DOG —— A dog that is eligible to compete for the title of champion and is being exhibited at AKC shows for that purpose.

STRIPPING —— Removing the outer coat by hand with the use of stripping knife.

LIST OF CREDITS

BREED	NAME	OWNER
Schnauzer	Ch. Helarry's Dark Victory	Larry Downey, Libertyville, Illinois
Wire Fox	Ch. Hetherington Druid Piper	Mr. and Mrs. Carruthers III, Cincinnati, Ohio
Wire Fox	Ch. Mark's Tey Brandy	Mario Migliorini, Wyoming, Delaware
Lakeland	Ch. Stingray of Derryabah	Mr. and Mrs. James A. Farrell, Jr. Darien, Connecticut
Scottish	Ch. Balachan Grenadier	Dr. T. Allen Kirk, Jr., Roanoke, Virginia
Sealyham	Ch. Alcide of Axe	Mrs. William W. Wimer III, Churchtown, Pennsylvania
West Highland White	Ch. Weaver's Drummond	Neoma and Jim Eberhardt, Santa Ana, California
Cairn	Ch. Caithness Colonel	Mrs. David W. Bryant, Bridgeport, Texas
Norwich	Ch. Longways Noel's Eve	Mrs. Emory G. Alexander, Haverford, Pennsylvania